I've been through the Fire

"MOMMA'S LITTLE GIRL"

I remember saying to my mom when I was thirty-four years old, "I was never anybody's little girl," she said, "You were always my little girl Shirley." The love I heard in those five little words made up for all of the times when I felt that nobody loved me.

She was only fourteen when she became pregnant with me. She had been enticed and seduced by a man ten years her senior, my daddy. He was a player. Spoiled by his granddaddy, who was the wealthiest man in the community, Black or White. The community, the church and the school carried his name, Sims Chapel Community, Sims Chapel Methodist Church and Sims Chapel School.

She turned fifteen March 9th, and I was born six months later, September 18th, 1941. She must have been his Christmas present. Can you imagine finding out on your fifteenth birthday that you were going to be a mother. I don't have to imagine it because I experienced the reality of being pregnant by a man who had raped me. An older man. He stole my virginity. A first date, fifteen, a senior in high school.

She and I had such high hopes for my future. I had just graduated with honors. Three scholarship offers, member of the honor society, student council and a 3.8 GPA. She and I had decided that I would attend Livingstone College in Salisbury, NC. Their offer paid my tuition. She had shared with Ms. Tanner, her employer, how her oldest child was going to college. She worked a half day five days a week, cleaning and cooking. She made ten dollars a week. "I want you to start paying me by the month, she said to Ms. Tanner, now that Shirley's going to college." She would sign that check and mail it to me, my room and board was forty dollars a month.

She was working in her garden when I finally got nerve enough to tell her. I knew she would be disappointed in me. I had known since missing my June period that I was pregnant. I'd learned that from her many times of pregnancy, seven children and pregnant with her eighth at thirty-two years old. She had given up on her future and was hoping that I would not fall into the same trap.

"She was supposed to be leaving for college in a few weeks Dr. Bull," as he confirmed that I was pregnant. "She wouldn't be having this baby if she was my daughter," he responded. "Come and I'll make the arrangements, young lady, get yourself dressed," as they walked into his office. Thank you Dr. Bull, "Come on Shirley, Dr. Bull made an appointment for us to see this doctor in Union tomorrow." We drove home in total silence.

I knew when she told Ben. I could hear him screaming and cussing, calling me and her names. "She ain't gonna be staying here," as he stormed out, walling his eyes at me. We both cried. Next day we went to Union to start the process. It took three trips. She drove me the first day and I drove by myself the next two days. I had just gotten driver's licenses. "You can drive yourself Shirley, somebody has to be here with these "chillum."

I was Ben's chauffeur. He had lost his driver's license for the third or fourth time for DUI's. He'd wake me up early Saturday morning to drive him on his route to sell his ball tickets. We'd always pick up a few of his drinking friends. They'd drink and cuss the whole time. I hated Saturday mornings. Sunday would be the same thing but included funerals sometimes two or three on that Sunday. We'd leave one before it's over to reach another before it was over. This was how my weekends were spent. I'd ask to use the car to go out with my friends, but that didn't happen. "You better get your ass somewhere and set down and get outta my face before I knock you outta it," was always his response.

One Saturday morning one of the men made an inappropriate gesture to me. I didn't know what to do or who to tell or if to tell. I asked my mom if she would tell him I couldn't drive him anymore. She would just look at me. She was just as frighten of him as I was. "Bennie, where did you find this little fresh chick?" the man said when Ben returned to the car. "That's my daughter, nigger." "Your daughter, then what the hell you doing having her drive you here like this?" The men were upset with him. They asked me to take them back where I had picked them up from.

I whimpered all the way to the house as he screamed and cussed that I'd better not say nothing to Helen. When he went to bed drunk as he did every Saturday morning, I pulled her to the side and told her what had happened. I don't know what she told him but that was the ending of my chauffeuring him on Saturday, but the funerals on Sunday continued.

He married my momma just before Mary Alice was borne. I was almost four years old. The Sims family was happy when she was borne, "she looks just like the Sims, they would say, I don't know who that other one look like, I ain't never believed she was Bennie's," Ms. Geneva would say. Thus was the beginning of the abuse from Ben and his family. I was always in somebody's way. "Git on outdoor somewhere and play," was an often statement screamed at me. I would try and get to my momma. It's the same spirit that try to keep me away from her today. I often say, "My daddy died, but his spirit didn't." I see it every time I try to get near my momma. The resentment is overwhelming sometimes.

Ben became my molester at an early age. It began as fondling. "Come here Gal," he would say, weaving his head to the side. That was the sign that he had been drinking. I thought he was calling me because he liked me. I was so hungry for attention. I missed the closeness of my mother. I had this before all of the others came into our lives. He would sit me on his lap and rub my legs until he reached my crouch. I would jump down thinking, "That doesn't feel right." One day he cornered me when no one was around. He grabbed me and jammed his finger in my crouch. I started to scream from the pain. He covered my mouth, "Shut up," he sneered. He moved the hand around my neck, "If you ever tell, you'll die, you hear me," he said. "Yes sir," crying.

I would slip away next door where my other grandmother lived. My mom and I lived there until she married Ben. My grandmamma didn't have a lot of time for me. She was taking care of my cousins, Della Mae. Della's mother died when she was seven months old and I was five months old. She was only seventeen when she died of pneumonia. I would cry when I had to go back to Ms. Geneva's house. They would tease and call me "Cry Baby." Ben would say, "She's crazy, ain't got a bitter sense," as he gave me that look that dared me to tell.

Marion and my momma were pregnant at the same time. Both by men much older than them. My cousin Bennie Mae, Momma's oldest sister's daughter, would tell how my daddy and Mr. Horace would come and rape them when no one was home. She would hide and watch between the cracks. They would rape them in the same room at the same time and dare them to tell. Of course no one every believed her. It was easier to believe they were "fast" girls than to believe they were being raped by older men in the neighborhood. No one believed me when I tried to tell.

I was sixty years plus when it began to manifest. My mother knew I was telling the truth. She allowed them to take her voice, as Ben and his family had always done. They convinced her that I was crazy and just trying to hurt the "family's name." I call it total recall.

"WHO STOLE MY DREAM?"

Total Recall,
Post Traumatic Syndrome Behavior

THE SEED

Your "SEED" Lord is crying for help.
They rape her, and sodomize her.
They molest her, and kill her.
They abuse her, and use her.
They handle her, and bruise her.
Why Lord, Why Lord?

They call me "Strong," I'm not.
They call me "smart, I'm not,
They call me "Shrewd," I'm not,
They call me Eve, I am.
The seed of God, I am.
They call me "Woman."

You blew the seed into man.
The seed gave him life.
You saw his need and supplied it.
Lord your "seed" is crying for help.
They work us and ask for more.
They leave their "seed" and then they flee.

Who can stand your wrath that touched your seed?
Created by you for man from your womb.
Who can touch and not be touched by your wrath.
Spare your prayers, morns, and your groans,
For there shall be gnashing of teeth and tearing of flesh
And ravishing of the mind as to reprobate and err
For to touch the seed of God is to cross the line
Where justice will not rob mercy and the redeeming love
For Your Seed Lord God of all host.
Sister Shirley Gray, A Saint of the Most High God © 2005

      It showed up as a personage dressed in black and I knew it was evil from the feel of my surroundings. "The Blood of Jesus Christ," I screamed. He fled but not before he touched me. I was in the home of my youngest son Steven and his wife Venita in Greenville, North Carolina. Steven, a ROTC instructor for the United States Air force at East Carolina University and Venita had just had their third child, a little girl, Nandi Adrianne Tugman. She was born on the fifteenth of January 2005. It was my plan to be there to witness her birth as I did Malik, their second child. He would be the first of my grandchildren I had witnessed, but it was not to be. I had an accident the week I had planned to leave.

      I was leaving Spartanburg Day School. They had invited me to exhibit my art. I had set everything up. I stopped at the red light. When it changed I accelerated but the car in front of me didn't move. I jammed the front end of my Cadillac into the rear of her SUV. My car scratched her bumper but destroyed my radiator to the tune of twenty-eight hundred dollars. The repairs took a week. Nandi was born and I am still in Spartanburg waiting for my car to be ready.

      I had been so blessed to be with Steven and his family since Johnnie died. They were stationed at Warner Robinsons Air Force base in Macon, Ga. One of my greatest thrills was being there for grandparent's day at Jamal's school. It was a challenge to get there. I had packed the night before. That was a good thing. I was scheduled to be the guest for Bill Drakes radio show from eight to nine am that morning. I woke up just a few minutes before the scheduled time and left home in a panic. Jamal's program was scheduled to begin at eleven O'clock. I made the show. I drove from Spartanburg to Macon in record-breaking time. It was worth every mile when I saw Jamal's face light up. He said that, "he loved his grandmother because she was smart, and loved him and brought him lots of things," I was one proud grandma. He was one proud grandson because I had traveled the farthest.

I missed Jamal's birth, Steven was stationed at Travis Air Force Base in California, and I was too busy trying to survive. I had lost my job at Greenville Hospital System. Johnnie wasn't working, as usual. I was struggling to keep my home. Hind sight tells me I should have gone. Steven carried hurt for my absence. He never told me but Laney, my stepdaughter did. It gave her a chance to talk about me not being at the birth of any of her children. She became pregnant with Anitra after Joe, her daddy, and I had separated. I was living in Spartanburg, SC. I would have been there if someone had informed me, just as I would have been to Grandma Delia and Uncle George's funeral if I had known of their deaths.

I missed the birth of Kesha and Kendall, Lamont and Teresa's twins. I had been there when early contractions began. They admitted her to Walter Reed Hospital in Washington, DC. Chante' Lamont Tugman, a United States Marine Master Gunnery Sergeant, and Teresa had been married about a year or more when they learned they were pregnant with twins. We were excited about getting twins in the family; their grandfather, Bynum Tugman was an identical twin, Bynum and Cummie Tugman; I had miscarried identical twins. My first pregnancy with my husband and their father, Joe Bynum Tugman.

I wanted more than anything to be with the twins when they were borne. I allowed my stepdaughter's jealousy not being there when her children were borne to stop me. I was working at the Greenville Hospital System when I got the call from Laney about Teresa being in the hospital. Lamont had moved her and her daughter Erica to live with Laney. It was mass confusion the entire time. Laney called me every day with complaints about Teresa and Erica.
I drove from Spartanburg, SC to Holly Ridge, NC, picked up Vivian, Teresa's mother whom I had never met, and on to Dale City, VA. After thirteen hours of driving we finally arrived. Vivian, Teresa's mama, drank beer and slept the entire trip. When I called her and asked if she wanted to ride with me, she said, "Hey, but I drink beer." That's alright with me, it's going in you not me," I answered. Teresa stayed in Walter Reed from July to September 1st when the twins were born.

When I returned home from Steve's I was hungry for some home cooked food, fresh vegetables and some starch. I stopped at the vegetable stand in Arkwright and bought some collard greens and fat back to season them. I had a pork roast in the freezer and prepared it to complete my meal of candied sweet potatoes and cornbread. As I was eating I began to feel a little dizzy and thought it to be just tired after those few days at Steve's and the long drive home. The break had been good for me by getting me away from myself.

I worked my business from my home. I had been pushing very hard to get this business where I wanted it. I knew the value of this art. I wanted to ride on the momentum that New York Life Insurance Company had left, the corporate sponsor of the exhibit, "Rising Above Jim Crow: The Paintings of Johnnie Lee Gray." They had bought one of the paintings for $100,000 after reneging on the contract. I used $60,000 to be into my home, bought and paid cash for my furniture and shared some with my sons, Lamont and Steve. Joe was in Nashville, TN and didn't get to share in the blessing.

My business has to pay for this home. I was working from four-thirty AM to one and two in the morning writing letters, making phone calls, and working to finish my first book. I needed to have the solace I find when traveling by myself, it gives me the opportunity to talk with God and listen to him.

At about two am in the morning I awaked nauseated barely making it to the bathroom that is in my bedroom. Seven hours later I was still on the bathroom floor too weak to lift my head and having chills. After talking to myself about not dying here in this big house by myself, I managed to drag myself to the bed. No one calls anymore or come to see me so it would be a while before I am missing and I'll be rotten by then, I thought.

I pulled myself up into my bed and continued to throw up in the bed when my phone began to ring. "It's nine' o'clock AM I thought, who could be calling me. "Hello, I said barely talking, I am so sick, help me." "Shirley, this is Decindy, I called to give you that information you needed to finish our taxes," she was saying over my plea for help. "Decindy I am sick, I've been sick all night," I said with a little more strength. I knew that this was my chance to get some help. "Have you called Grandma Helen," she said. "Decindy, I'm sick," I said almost pleading. "OK Shirley, I'm going to call Grandma Helen and tell her that you'll sick, Ok," she said, with it finally sinking in, that I'm sick. The phone rang almost as soon as she hung up. "Shirley, Decindy said that you down there sick. What you doing down there sick by yourself? I've got this baby and you being sick I don't need to bring him down there," she was saying, justifying her reason.

This baby is her great- grand son Christopher, my niece Charlita's son. She is the daughter of my sister Joyce. If it had been anybody else's baby, she would have brought that babysitting to an end. Just as she had done when Decindy brought her children, our brother's wife, who was in prison for trafficking drugs. Or as she did when my children or Mary Alice's children came around. She was worse than Ben. He made it known that he did not want my children or me in the house. I made the down payment on that house after the foreclosure.

Nor did they want Ronnie and Suzette, Mary Alice's children whose social security checks made the monthly payments and Mary Alice paid the house off. Nor did she want Sandra's children, Kenneth, Jr. and Michelle, who was incarceration in the state women's correctional center in Columbia, SC. However, it was okay for her and her family, she, Charlita, Travis and whoever else she invited to come every Sunday and many times through the week.

"Call 911 and see if you can get somebody to come and help you, I've got this baby, you know," she said again as I was throwing up again. "I'll call 911, but I don't know how they are going to get me because I'm all locked up. But they will figure it out," I was saying as I hung up the phone. I called 911 and told them of my dilemma and about me being locked down. "Try to get to the door ma'am and if you can't call us back," the dispatcher was saying.

I rolled out of bed and crawled to the breakfast area, pulled myself up to a chair for support and pushed it with me hanging on. I pushed until I got to the front door and unlocked it. I tried to return to the bathroom but gave out of strength. I peed in my clothes on to the floor. I was embarrassed. I was not dressed, hair unkempt and the bathroom was a mess. I had puked, bowels moved, since one am. It was now nine am.

As she found underwear and a gown for me the phone began to ring. "The answering machine will pick it up," I said to the attendant. "Shirley, the voice said, we are trying to figure out how to get you from down there, Helen said you are sick," it was Pat with her "what's with her now" attitude. "Answer that please and let her know you are here," I said a little embarrassed that I did not have family that had time to see about me. My children, all boys, lived out of state. I always listed my mother as closest of kin.

I spent the entire day in the emergency room with them giving me fluids and blood pressure medicine. I know it was a heart attack or a stroke. If they had ordered a chemistry test they would have known also. I lost my equilibrium for almost two months and no energy. This was the beginning of six months of hell and back. After being at Helen's house I was more tired being there than I would be in my own home.

"That Big O House"

I bought my home in August of 2004 after selling one of my paintings for $100,000. The fifty thousand I put down qualified me for a loan; the greedy weren't going to leave that money on the table. They found me a lender. A pirate mortgage at eight point nine percent interest rate. Interest rate were as low as three percent for perfect credit which I didn't have but I had some money.

Each morning she would lay some of her clothes out for me and each night give me a pair of her pajama's to sleep in. The "big four" started coming in after two o'clock, one by one. "How is Shirley," they would ask my mama. I wondered if they thought I wasn't capable of telling how I felt. I knew if I could get home I would feel better. Each day was a greater struggle. The negative vibes in the house impeded my recovery. Finally I asked if I could go to the comforts of my own home. I was longing for my spa and my big comfortable queen size bed.

They all had come to see "this big house Shirley done bought." This stay gave my mother the opportunity to express herself about buying this "big house." "I just believe you moved too fast buying that house. I don't understand why you have to have a house that big anyway," she would say with her worried look. She never asked, what are your plans or your goals. Nor what are your feelings. It always was concerns about whether I'm going to fail. I am one of the conversational pieces for the weekly Sunday dinner. The other is what's wrong with the church and the people in it, who died, who went to jail and how bad everyone is doing, especially the young ones.

I had my house warming September 18th, my birthday. It was a glorious time for me. Steven and Lamont and their families were here. I was excited being in a brand new home. "Shirley, Lita and I was talking about you giving a house warming, she said and I agree with her, that why would you give a house warming and you've been housekeeping for thirty years, people might think you are looking for them to buy you something." I haven't celebrated a birthday in years; please let me do this. You don't have to come and you don't have to bring anything," I was saying getting a bit upset with her thinking that Lita, my niece, knew more about what I should do than I do. I had the house warming, many came and many brought beautiful gifts. They came but brought nothing.

"Remembering"

This total recall is a healing process for me. God in his infinite wisdom introduced me to the many personalities I'd developed. They protected me. I had internalized the traumatic experiences. The experience transfers from the conscience mind to the subconscious mind. It controls your life unconsciously. An incident triggers the subconscious mind to transfer to the conscience mind. You unconsciously transform into the personality that protects you. I didn't learn this in a psychology class. The Holy Spirit taught this to me.

I remember being lost in a zoo. We were stationed in Boise, Idaho. We were with a group of people. I became separated from them. I remember the smell of the Polar Bears and being very frightened. Then the pain between my legs. The pain like when you hurt your crouch on the middle bar of a boy's bicycle. I don't remember the people or why we were there. I remember the pain and the smell of the Polar bears.

"Shirley I never took you to a zoo," my mother said. I tried telling the story. "But Helen, I said in defense of the experience, maybe I was with someone you trusted." "If you were only three when this happened I would have noticed because I was still bathing you. You were just sick Shirley. That didn't happen to you, you were just sick," she said dismissing me with a disgust sigh. I walked away hurt. I believed that she had believed me when I told her. It was just me and her.

There was no understanding of what was going on with me. They labeled me as mental ill and put me on the mental ward, March 9, 1979, my mother's birthday. There was an uncontrollable anger against Joe, my ex-husband and Ben, my daddy.

"O baby don't you weep, o mother don't you mourn."

"The first date"

I was raped by Isaac Crawford on my first date. I was sixteen years old. A man who was five to six years my senior. I never told because I knew I would be blamed. I was blamed for many things just because I was the oldest. "And there's Shirley and she's the oldest," my daddy would snarl. I could never figure out what being the oldest had to do with anything. I remembered the pain. It was the same pain I remembered when I was lost at the zoo. I thought we were near a railroad track. The noise sounded as if a train was passing. He told me to fix my clothes. I looked around and there was no train tracks. Maybe the noise was my screams going internal. He took me home without saying a word.

"You got to marry me, crying, you've got to marry me. You stole my virginity." "Shut up bitch, how was I supposed to know you'd never screwed, what'd you think I came for, you ugly bitch," he spitted out. I cried silently the remaining way home. "Git out and you "better not tell anybody or I'll come back and get some more," he said as he drove off.

I felt like a wounded animal with nowhere or no one to turn to. I came into the house. Everyone was sleeping. I found my way into the room where all the "chillums" slept. I didn't turn on lights. I knew every inch of the room. There were only beds with boxes that held our clothes under the beds. I pulled out the box with the panties and got a clean pair. I wrapped the ones I had on in the skirt I'd just pulled off. I got in bed with only my under wear. I hid my clothes under the pillow. In the morning I got rid of them.

I didn't want to get up. I was in so much pain. I felt as if my insides were torn out. I bled as if I was having my period, when I realized it was my period. I became horrified. Suppose I am pregnant, I had heard the older women talking that you can get pregnant if you have sex just before you have your period. Anxiously I waited for my next month's period. I began walking normally after a couple of days. Helen had noticed me walking wide legged and asked why was I walking like that. "On I'm on my monthly and you know how those sanitary napkins irritate me," I said as I continued doing whatever I was doing. She never asked about it again.

I became obsessed with the thoughts that this man had to marry me. I had promised myself that the first man that I would have sex with would be my husband. I wanted to be able to walk down the aisle in a white dress just like the "white" girls. I thought all "white" girls were virgins. Just like I thought all "white folks" were smart. They had all of the money and the good jobs, so they had to be smart. Money was the only thing they had that I didn't have. Who wants to be "white" anyways? I have enough problems with this fair colored skin. My sisters and relatives always commented about my complexion, as if I was responsible for being "red." I'm going to be smart just like them so I can get me a good job and live in the same kind of house they live in became my dream.

I would inquire of Isaac through my "friend" Dorothy Walker, whose boyfriend, James Means introduced to me. I met James on Short Wofford Street in downtown Spartanburg, SC where all of the "Black" businesses where. The Black's hung out on Saturday. I remember my grandmother and my mother's older sisters coming home on Saturday night in a cab. They would always smell of beer, cigarettes and the nightlife. My mother couldn't go because she had to watch after me. My grandma said, "If you make your bed hard then you've got to sleep in it." I was her hard bed.

This was the meeting place for the leaving and returning of the boys and girls attending Camp Harry Daniel, in Eloree, SC. He was there to pick up his brother Archie and I was there to pick up Mary Alice and "Poochie," my sister and brother. The conversation was causal until he asked if he could come see me. I said yes. I gave him directions to my house. Dorothy and I were standing in her front yard when he drove by in this big dump truck hauling used bricks from one of the buildings downtown.

Dorothy was an only girl and the younger of two brothers. She was the little pretty girl with the long hair in the community. Her grandfather owned the house we were renting. This gave her a sense of superiority to me. She took every opportunity to express it. I was the first of the three of us; she, Ruth Morrow and I to get pointed toed shoes. Helen's white woman had vouched for her to have an account at Bomars. Their mothers had to put there's on lay-away.

"Why did you get pointed toe shoes with feet as large as yours? You need small feet like me and Ruth for pointed toes shoes to look good on your feet," she said with a sneer on her face. I had been so proud having on a brand new pair of shoes from an expensive store. She was jealous and I didn't recognize it. I just wanted to be her friend and be accepted by her. She always hurt my feelings. She came to my house one time while I was changing the beds, somebody peed in the bed every night, and sometimes more than one would be wet.

The beds hadn't been made all day with the covers thrown back to dry. Someone had given us some white material from somewhere. I had hemmed them for sheets and was about to put them on the beds when she came in. "What's that awful smell, pew, how can you stand it in here? I'll come back when you finish because I can't stand that smell," as she was leaving to go back to her house.

I was upset that she would come before I got the sheets changed and leave with the attitude she left with. All I had to do was flip the mattress over to the dry side. Put fresh sheets on and the odor would be gone. On Saturday I would let them air dry with the windows opened. Then there was the bucket with diapers soaking. Off course this was my job.

James stopped and talked and as he was leaving he said, "I'm coming to see you tonight." "Okay," I said, assuming he was talking to me. That night we had Usher Board Meeting at Dot Wilke's house when there was a knock on the door. "Wait a minute young man, I'll get her. "Shirley there's a young man out here asking for you." "Okay, I said looking around at Dorothy, it must be James Means, you know he said he'd see me tonight, I'd forgotten about us having Usher Board meeting tonight." "Hello James, we'll be finished with our meeting in a few minutes if you want to wait outside for me," I was saying, greeting him with a big smile pleased that he'd come to see me." "O' I thought the other girl was Shirley and that you was Dot," he said with a twist in the corner of his mouth. I knew he was lying. "Oh it's Dorothy that you want, not me, I'll go and get her, Dorothy it's you that he wants," as I returned trying not to disturb the meeting. "Okay Shirley but I don't know what he wants with me," she said and I knew she was lying also.

James and Dorothy became a couple. That lie that he told that night was the beginning of a nightmare for Dorothy. They later married. I wouldn't wish the life he gave her on my worst enemy. He introduced his friend Isaac Crawford to me. Sex is all his friend had in mind when he took me out. I doubt if he remembered my name. I remembered his. I never forgot what he took from me. Later he became a police officer in New York and was killed in the line of duty.

"The unexplained Nightmares"

I would wake up in a cold sweat feeling as if I were dying. I could not understand the nightmares. I thought it was God's way of punishing me for what had happened. I always felt bad and worthless. Miss Geneva, my daddy's mother and his sister Fannie Mae said I would never be nothing. I guess this is what happens when you are nothing. What had I done that would cause God to make me be nothing, and what is nothing?

"You thank you something but you ain't; you thank you so smart but you ain't; you thank you looking good but you don't; you ain't nothing but an old red/yellow dog; you didn't come from nothing because your mama didn't come from nothing. You ain't never had no sense you'd the craziest old thing I'd ever seen wit' your red self. Shirley has book sense but she doesn't have common sense she just let folks use her. I don't worry about Mary Alice, she can take care of herself, but not Shirley she just let people tell her anything, like Dot Walker. She'll do anything Dot Walker tell her to do. These are statements I grew up hearing and returned a thirty-three year old adult hearing once again. It's as if they had been stuck in a time zone and hadn't grown to maturity in all of these years.

Everything that happened to us in the past shapes our today. If we were happy in the past can we be happy in the future? Yes, if we realize that happiness is determined by our circumstances and it is temporary. What if we were sad, does that mean that we will always be sad? Sadness like happiness is a temporary condition and is only temporary. I've learned through my many different experiences in life that the only things for certain are life and death and what we do between the two is living.

As I began to reminisce over my life I can find many rainbows and many storms. When we are in the mist of the storm we cannot see the rainbow but we must know that there is a rainbow coming at the end of the storm. After the rainbow comes the freshness of the air, the rejuvenation of life to the plants and animals and the moistening of the dry earth. It returns to the clouds in the form of condensation and the cycle begins again. So is life. It is a cycle. I ask, "have your cycle of life been broken by the cares of this world?"

All rains are not raging and rainbows are not always visible. Some are drizzles and scattered showers. Storms are different in that some are raging rains with thunder and lightings. Some are Hugo's and Andrews. Some are earthquakes and floods and some are landslides and rockslides. Rains are refreshing and restoring, storms are destructive and sometimes fatal but both produces new life.

After the rainfall comes the clean smell of the air, the movement of the earthworm, the blossoming of the flowers, the singing of the birds, and the awakening of nature. After the storm comes the cleaning up of the destruction, the search for the lost, the rejoicing for the survivors, and the rebuilding of that which was destroyed. The latter becomes greater than the first and we move on.

What kinda man you gonna marry?
A rich man, poor man, doctor lawyer,
What kinda car you gonna drive?
A-model, T-model, V-8 Ford
What kinda house you gonna live in?
Big house, little house, masters quarters

What you gonna be when you grow up?
Housewife, teacher, preacher' wife.
How many children you gonna have?
12345678910

Black woman, Black woman
Can't you be what you want to be?
No Madam, No madam
I can't be what I want to be
No housewife, teacher, or preacher's wife.

Black woman, Black Woman
You can be what you want to be.
T'is so Madam, T'is so.
I can be what I want to be.
Doctor, lawyer, CEO

Oh Black woman, Black women,
Don't fool yourself, with your mind so high,
Dem white folks ain't gonna give you place up there
They need you to pap their young so they can make their mark
So be what they want you to be,
Housewife, Maid, or laundry worker

Mama, Mama why can't it be
It can be my child, just wait and pray
Mama, Mama, Mama
I've been waiting and I've been praying
I've been learning and I've been doing
They make the money and I take the blame
Dem white folks done took my place again.

Glory, glory halleluiah, glory, glory halleluiah
My eyes has seen the coming of the Lord
His truth is marching on.
I can be a doctor, lawyer, CEO
I have a dream opened the door

I am a doctor, lawyer, CEO
Nurse, Teacher, Cytotech.
Writer, Actress, [Astronaut
Engineer, carpenter, jackhammer too.

Comment [SG]:

No one can steal your dream
It changed with the times
No one can take your hope
It's the substance of Faith the size of a mustard seed
Dream on, Black Sister, Dream on.   Shirley Sims Gray ©2003

And He's gone"

   I graduated from high school at the ripe old age of sixteen. My mother registered me in
first grade at age four turning five that September 18th 1946. Bennie Ervin Sims, Jr., the third
child was borne March 13th 1946 five months before school began. My mother is now a twenty
year old with a four and a half year old, me, a two year old, Mary Alice and now another baby,
Bennie's first son, and a husband still living with his mother. We all slept in the front bedroom.
Ben, Helen and Mary Alice in one bed. I slept in the baby's crib with my legs hanging out
between the railings, and another baby made things a little crowded.

   Ben had to go away to the chain gang for DUI and while he was gone Helen found us a
little house across the railroad track that someone had built there. I thought it was the prettiest
house in all of the community and it had a front porch. Everything was so peaceful while he was
gone. No more weekend fights and no more drinking and bringing drunk men home with him
that's always looking at you with evil in their eyes. Sometimes they didn't wait to get outside
before making a comment about "that pretty little thing with them big legs." I hated weekend.
All the men got drunk and drove their cars like crazy men. Ben, my daddy, and Southern, my
mama's brother were the wild ones with the drinking and driving. Most of all, we didn't have to
be in Miss Geneva's house anymore with her, Fannie Mae, Ben's sister, and Jackie boy, her
bastard son.

   We couldn't play. You had to sit in the little chairs she had assigned us and stay quite.
When we got older, Helen would leave us with her, she would make us all, including Jackie Boy
crochet. It was always boring. We would argue about looking at one another, then she made us
take a nap. She had certain ways for you to lie so you wouldn't be touching one another. I'd
always wanted to stay home and did when I turned thirteen. I would use this time to clean the
house while everyone is gone.

   Ben returned home from the chain gang and raised hell because Helen had moved us out of
his mama's house. For the first time Helen stood her grounds. "You can go back home with
your mama but these chillums and me going to stay here," she said with pride. She found the
house and talked the landlord into renting it to her. I don't know what the terms were I just
know that we were finally a family living on our own. Shortly after Ben returned his old habits
returned also. Helen getting pregnant with the fourth child, now it's me seven, Mary Alice four,

"Poochie" two and a half and a new baby, Glenda Patricia Sims, July 9th, 1948, Helen was twenty-two years old.

One Saturday morning my daddy brought a man to the house with him. While they were gone he returned. My daddy would take my mother to the grocery store and the children down to our grandmother's. I would stay to clean the house. I looked up. There he stood in the doorway with a five -dollar bill in his hand. I knew this was danger. I dropped the broom and began to back away. Never running but slowly backing through the house. He slowly walked toward me, coaching me to take the money. I got to the back door and turned to run. He turned to go back through the house to head me off. My daddy and mama drove up.
I ran to their car. She was screaming, "Did he say anything to you," she yelled in my face. "No, I lied. I was more frighten of her than I was him.

She seemed to be seven feet tall and had the world's largest hands that could cover your face or your butt with one slap. It was never just one slap. My daddy took the man away. I never saw him again. It was never mentioned again. Many things happened that was never mentioned, as if it never happened.

"Alone and lonely"
"I'm just a little girl, a loner. I always felt alone.
I was never anyone's little girl.
Who's gonna take time with me.
Who's going to show me things that little girls should know.
I had a friend that I talked too.
She taught me things
How to read, how to sing.
How to watch and listen to the birds.
They sing out their agenda for the day.
How to watch the movement of nature and know that a storm was on the way.
I could hear mama or my grand mama call my name.
But I would not answer. It was my secret place to read and talk to my friend.
I would tell her my dreams. She wouldn't call me dumb or laugh.
I was going to be a famous person with lots of money.
I would build a large house and hire white folks to be my maids.
I was going to have the biggest car in the world with a driver.
My husband was going to be tall, dark, and handsome.
We were going to make love just as they did in the Modern Romance books I read.
I was going to have five boys because I hated girls.
As the voice got closer, I would come from my hiding place on the other side of the house.
My Mother would scream, "Didn't you hear me calling you girl, git in this house?" My grandmother would say, "I bet ya she was somewhere with her head stuck in a book, gonna grow up and keep a nasty house cause she'd be somewhere with her head stuck in a book".
Shirley Sims Gray © 2005

I was always glad when the summers was over and time to return to school. Miss Walker could make the best soup and peanut butter sandwiches. The schoolhouse was two rooms and a kitchen in a wooden building with a big potbelly stove in each classroom. It was the building my great-granddaddy had given the community and was named Sims Chapel School after him.

Lunchtime the classrooms became the dining room. There were first, second and third grades in one room and fourth, fifth and six grades in the other room. We were about thirty in the whole school. Miss Levels and Mrs. Robinson were our teachers and they were tough. Each morning we had to recite our timetables and had to know them through the twelfth before we could get out of the third grade. If you heard us, you would think we were singing. One time one is one, one time two is two we recited on and on with rhythm.

We read with rhythm, Winky, Dick, and Jane became my friends. I loved Winky. He was the pet monkey who always got into trouble. I would read aloud at home preparing for school the next day because I did not want to miss not one word. Miss Levels give you a lick for each word you missed. I would read over and over until my Dad would scream out, "Put that damn book down, I'm sick and tired of Winky. Winky, Winky, Winky, go to bed."
Sometimes my mother would speak up for me, other times she would gently take the book and say, "It's alright you did good."
Spelling was the last thing of the school day. We would stand in line and spell as she called the word. I always wanted to be first in line. You had to earn your place in the line. I was second in line and Betty Brewton was always first. One night I did not finish my studying for the spelling because I had to go to bed. Miss level called my word, "Coffee Shirley," I thought for a while, I don't remember seeing that word so I spelled it as I heard it. "K-o-f-f-e-e, coffee",
"Get to the end of the line Shirley". I began to cry as I moved to the end of the line. When it was time to come up for the licks, I went to the end of the line. As each one received their lick, the line moved up closer to Miss Levels. I did not move.

"Come on up Shirley, you will get one lick because you only missed one," Miss Level's said trying to coach me into coming up. Moving to the end of the line was enough humiliation for one day and now she wants to add insult on insult. I would not budge. She started toward me, and I took off running, round and round the room. "Catch her, catch her," Miss Levels cried, no one could stop me. I fought back. Finally, my cousin tackled me but not without a good fight. I scratched and kicked and hollered until Miss Levels grabbed me with those big old arms of hers. All I could do was squirm. That was one of the worst spankings I ever received from Miss Levels. From now on, I am going to study my lesson come hell or high waters. I would start my lesson as soon as I got home so I could finish before my Daddy called bedtime. He came home from work, ate, read the paper and went to bed whether it was still daylight or not. Whenever he'd wake from his first round of sleep he'd make everybody else go to bed.

The Nurse from the city came to give us our vaccinations. It was cold that morning. My mother had dressed me in a red snow suit. She bought this for me in Boise Idaho. I was late for some reason and when I walked in, they were waiting for me. The nurse said, "Oh look at her, she looks just like Santa Claus, you are next," the nurse said. She had on her blue and white stripped dress with a red cross on the front of it. I knew who she was and why she was there. She *had been there before. I'll never forget that big red cross on her dress. I began backing up until I reached the door and out of it, I dashed.*

I ran to my Uncles Gilbert's store next door. He was my hero. He was the tallest man I knew, and the same complexion I was. I knew he would help me. He had locked up and gone inside to eat breakfast.   He heard the screams and saw the crowd running after me, Miss Levels, the nurse, my cousins Eddie, Della Mae, and Barbara Jean. I was running round and round the store. Uncle Gilbert stepped outside of his store and grabbed me as I had circled the third time. I knew I was safe. Uncle Gilbert carried me back to the schoolroom and let me sit on his lap while I took my shots. I promised him I would be a big girl so I could get the big Baby Ruth that he had waiting for me.

At the end of the school year, we would be busy practicing for our operetta. The whole community would come out. May Day had been a success; Betty Brewton went to the spelling contest and won because she spelled "opportunity," we all had had our shots, and it was time to kick off shoes and run through the red dirt.

What a time, what a time?

It was the beginning of summertime,
Camp time, and gardening time,
Harvesting time, peach- picking time,
And daydreaming time.
It was the time to reminisce and
Time for the relatives up North to visit down South,
It was lemonade time, and fresh tomatoes from the vine time,
It was watermelon time and cantaloupe time,
It was corn and okra with green tomatoes time,
Fresh string beans and new potatoes,
It was a happy time, a carefree time,
It was three-digit temperature,
What a time, what a time?   Shirley Sims Gray © 2005

Miss Levels would dismiss for recess and sometimes for the remaining of the afternoon playing. She would play ball, shoot marbles, jump rope and tan your butt good for fighting. She whipped you for fighting in school and out of school. She would sometimes park her car midways until she thought everyone was home. I was always glad when she did that because I did not like the fights. They picked on me and called me names and I would go home crying every day. I earned the name "crybaby." I would escape in my books. I could be wherever I wanted to be and be whoever I wanted to be. I could daydream and tune out my surroundings; they would never be anybody important to me. I was going to be famous one day and everyone would love me.

I had made it to the second room learning math, English, and History. Mrs. Robinson was the teacher. She was so young and pretty. I really wanted to please her. I studied even harder than I did for Miss Levels, plus she didn't spank. She left that to Miss Levels, the Principal. Being in the fifth grade was so cool. I could be the nine-year-old and best of all I was the youngest in the class. All of the boys liked me and looked after me. At home, I was the oldest of five, Joyce Elaine, October 8th 1950. I began to get oldest responsibilities; helping with the baby, changing diapers, watching the younger ones, stirring the beans, making corn bread, laying the pattern, cutting out the pattern, doing all of the finger works such as hemming, braiding hair, watching the baby, watching the baby and watching the babies. Helen was twenty-four.

"My Promotion"

My mother was the seamstress in our small community. It was our bread and butter money. She would be up at five every morning to fix breakfast for Ben and get him off to work. Then she would get us up to get ready for school. It was always hot grits and whole cake bread. We would leave for school. My mother would clean our little four room modest house and began her day on the sewing machine. She would take care of my brother, Poochie, and my sister Pat and Joyce. That became my task when I came home from school. My mom would sew until the wee hours if it were a holiday. She would make four and five dresses a day. At nine years old, I became her assistance. She taught me how to lay the pattern and cut out the fabric. I used that skill in college and made dresses for the girls for a fee. I would do well making dresses for graduation.

I joined the 4-H Club in the fifth grade. Chickens were my first project. Thereafter it was sewing. Raising chicken was no joke. Miss Cammie Claggett was the home demonstration agent over the 4-H Club. She was almost white in complexion but not white enough to pass. We always heard that her daddy was a "white man". She was a big boisterous lady that would fill a room with her presence. She worked hard to get us girls into college and worked to get us scholarships. She would have countywide fashion shows for us to model the clothes we had made. She was good times. We baked cookies, and learned to prepare balanced meals, how to garden, harvest and preserve the fruits. We would enter booth competition at the county fair and exhibit our bakes and our preservative. The boys would display their cows and pigs and different farming skills. The 4-H club was an inspiration to me to excel in all of my doings and to do them as if you are in a contest to win.

We were so happy running this house. I didn't have to hide anymore to read and I was helping Helen. We would sit at night after getting all the children to sleep and listen to our favored radio shows; "Our Gal Sunday", "Inner Sanctions", "The Fat Man", "Ma and Pa Perkins", and others. I can't remember being so happy helping to cook and raise the babies and not being fussed at and called stupid and fussed at for being the oldest. Miss Geneva and Fannie Mae would come visit and the mood would change every time. She always could tell my Mother how to arrange our house and what she needed to do about me. She would say "I don't know what you gonna do with Shirley, she' so fast going around exposing herself". I never knew, what the hell she was talking about. What was I exposing?

Ben came home and all of the fun left. He would come in from work, eat and go to bed. We had to be quite not to disturb him. I would get so excited listening to the stories that he would threaten to make me go to bed. I wished he had never come home. I did not go with Helen to see him while he was on the chain gang. I did not go to visit Miss Geneva and Fannie Mae either. Soon after he came home we moved to Miss Granny Minnie Keenon's house. It was a better house and it had a commercial toilet stool in the outside toilet. Ben was on the chain gang again.

The chain gang was no joke. The men wore chains around there ankles. They had to learn how to dress and undress with the chains still around their ankles. They were housed up like hogs lying around on top of each other. They had to wear black and white strip pants and shirts.
They were a scary bunch of men chained down with balls on the chain. The men were treated less than human. Why would anyone keep going back to that lifestyle is beyond my comprehension. Helen got pregnant during one of those" slip a ways" with Jacqueline April 8th 1951, I was ten and Helen was twenty-five.

Ben got off the chain gang before Jackie was borne and we moved from Miss Keenon's to Miss Walker's house. Down the hill from Miss Keenon's house. We hand carried the furniture all day. When Ben got home, he got a truck and moved the refrigerator and stove. That night she gave birth to Jackie, another girl.

A few months later she said to Mary Alice and me, "We are all going to the clinic today and get our polio shot, they are giving them today to children and pregnant mothers," she said with a little reservation. "I ain't tending to no more babies," my sister Mary Alice start screaming, It's nuff of us already, I don't want no brother or sister, it already nuff of us." She ran out the front door and sat under the pear tree in our front yard crying. She stayed out there until we got ready to leave for the clinic.

Helen had her drivers' license now after trying seven times. Finally the patrol officer said, "Ma'am I'm going to give you your driver's license before you have this baby here. She was pregnant with Sandra Belinda, borne August 19th 1953. I was twelve and Helen was twenty-seven with six girls and one boy. Her husband was on the chain gang again.

Ben was one of the few men with a car so he was like the chauffer for the crowd and that made his popular with the women and envied by the men. He would always have a carload of women riding around in our neighborhood, and in our neighborhood liquor houses and café. This is what kept him on the chain gang, driving drunk. Liquor, Women and fast cars was his MO and a house full of chillum was extra baggage to his image. He'd been a "stone" gangster if it had not been for all of us girls and there were more to come.

MY "CHILLUMS"

O where O where are my chillum,
O where O where can they be?
First there was one, then two and more.
God gave him what he liked the most

Girls, Girls, Girls, and more Girls.
Jessie, the first, but not by Helen
Shirley the second, first for Helen
Mary Alice, third and choice
Patricia the fourth and O she's "Black"
Joyce the fifth and the feistiest
Jacqueline the sixth and the sneakiest
Sandra the seventh and says Daddy
Angela the eighth and the slowest, they thought
Please don't forget Barbara
Somewhere between Mary Alice and Me
She and her mother Nancy were our neighbors
O sons, O sons, where are you?
Bennie Jr. followed you to the grave
Albert's out of Jail and preaching the Word
Ricky, the last, is following your legacy
He belongs to the State just like you did.   Shirley Sims Gray © 2005

   The little girl across the street would come over and play with Mary Alice and Me. We never liked her because she always said she was our sister. It was alright with me but not Mary Alice. She would beat her up, make her eat dirt, and send her home crying, "Now that'll teach her with her ugly self, Miss Geneva said she ain't our sister and she ought to know," she would say almost with tears. Mary Alice was not going to allow anyone to take her place. She was the Sims' favored little girl and nothing or no one was going to change that. When the Northern relatives came into town they would always bring her something, give her money, sit her on their laps and tell her how pretty she was. I stood somewhere in a corner dying for someone to notice me.

   Mary Alice would always have a big Christmas because they, the Sims, would all buy for her. Dolls, tea sets, tricycles, and bunches of pretty new clothes. When I would come around to look at all of the stuff she had they told her she didn't have to share with me. They bought it for her and not me. Mary Alice would let me play with her things when they weren't around. If they came around while we were playing she would take them from me, hit me and run to them crying that I'd tried to take her toys. They would pick her up and take her and the toys away while fussing at me for "trying to take this "baby's stuff." I had to give up whatever I had when she and "Jackie Boy" came around whether it was there's or mine.

   I learned that the pony that Ben shipped from Boise, Idaho was 'Jackie Boys" and not mine. We'd talked about it many times about how Ben paid more for the shipping than he did the pony. I remembered the pony as one of my good memories of Boise, Idaho and now she's taken that away. "I wished you hadn't told that one Helen, it was one of the few good memories I had about Boise and the two old "white" men that were our neighbors. I used to go over to their house all of the time. They would play the fiddle for me and sing to me. I know they are dead because they were old men then. Why did you let me go to those men's house by myself when I

was just a little girl? I asked for the first time. "You d' the one that always wanted to go over there Shirley and they liked you so I'd let you go over there," defensively.

Comment [SG]: Begin editing.

I walked away remembering that they had a closet that I was always curious about. "What's in that door," I would ask them. "O you can't open that door it's something in there that'll get you," they would say. I don't get a good feeling now when I think about those two old "white" men. I remember the pump outside of their house where we got water. I thought that was the neatest thing, pump, pump, pump and finally the water came clear and clean. It was always more than the bucket could hold. They would let it spill over into the trough for the animals. There were no trees just bushes blowing around and the windstorms blowing sand in your eyes. They were always there to help get the sand out of my eyes and off my clothes. "You've got to learn how to cover your eyes Shirley when the wind blows the sand, don't you gonna always get sand in your eyes," they would tell me.

When he returned home from the chain gang off course babies started coming all over again. Dr. Pettis told Ben that he needed to sign so they could tie her tubes because she didn't need to have any more babies. Ben wouldn't sign, "I ain't signing a damn thing and you bet' in not do nothing to her. You do that and she won't be no good no more," he said angrily. "Mr. Ben your wife is young enough to have ten more babies, you need to stop this because it's jeopardizing her health," Dr. Pettis pleaded with him. "I ain't studying that shit, you better not do nothing to her," he said as he left the clinic.

Dr. Pettis and her husband had moved her from New Orleans, LA. To practice their medicine here in Spartanburg, SC with their Uncle, DR. J. C. Bull. He was one of the three Black doctors in Spartanburg, the others, Dr. Marion and William Douglas brothers. She was a general Practitioner and he was the Dentist. They built Bull's Clinic and a drugstore next door where her brother was the pharmacist. They were the richest Black folks in town except for Mr. Ernest Collins who owned most everything on Liberty Street and lived in a big house outside of town. He owned a hotel with a restaurant and liquor store inside, a funeral home, service station, houses, The Victor Tavern, a nightclub, buses, the bluebird cab plus he was a bails bondsman.

Miss Geneva used his service as a bails bondsman quite often. When Ben would get in jail she'd just call Mr. Collins and he would know what to do. "Judge this man's has ten or eleven chillum and he don't need to be locked up in jail but on his job Monday morning, can you lower his bail to just a fine Sir?" Mr. Collins would appeal to the night judge. "Ernest you been getting this man out of jail for as long as I've been here and this is his fourth or fifth offense, he's gonna make a lot of time this time so you go tell his mama her money won't work this time. Tell her to spend it on his chillums while he's gone to jail, because he's going for a while," the judge said.

Ben was gone for the longest this time. It was almost five years before there was any more babies, Albert McKinley, January 23rd, 1957 the same day one of the Queens sons were born, Angela Regina, January 29th, 1959 and Ricky Jerome May 22nd 1961, I was twenty and Helen was thirty-five. The tenth pregnancy with Ricky almost killed her; he weighed ten pounds and thirteen ounces. She had not prepared for this baby, no diapers or anything. Our neighbor

Mr. Brady Cureton had lost his wife during childbirth. Helen kept comparing herself to Mrs. Cureton and was afraid that this was going to happen to her also. Dr. Pettis had her on heart medication and a strict diet and the medication fed the baby, she said. She was afraid to go to the outside toilet for a bowel movement. She said, "It felt like that the baby would just fall out of my womb because he was so heavy."

I came home from college and stayed two weeks to help out. I had to get back to school to prepare for my finals. She had called to tell me that she was having a few problems with Mary Alice. I prompt her to tell me what trouble. Mary Alice was pregnant also. "She wasn't gonna be having no baby with her chillums," is what she told Dr. Bull when they ended my pregnancy. Fate has a way of winning anyway.

I Stopped Crying
I won't cry and let you know
I won't feel and then I won't cry
Went it hurt I'll just frown then you'll never know
How bad it hurts when I am crying.

I'll stop crying and maybe it won't
I'll stop crying and you'll never know
So don't give me something to cry for
Because I won't cry then you'll never know
How bad it hurts when I am crying.

I can't cry and you don't know
How soft my heart is and you'll never know
You may leave or even die
And I ain't crying and you don't know
How bad it hurts cause I won't cry.   *Shirley Sims Gray © 2003*

By the time I turned sixteen this ugly duckling had turned into a shapely swam. Men would approach me with all kinds of propositions. I couldn't understand what I was doing to make this happen. All I wanted was to be loved and if this was love I didn't want it. During the summer after my graduation I went out with one of the most popular guys in the school to a house party. Everyone that was somebody was at this party. I was having such a good time dancing, laughing and drinking for the first time.

The party was over about two am. Everything had gone well so far. He drove into my driveway and thanked me for going to the party with him. Just as he was about to kiss me I heard this loud scream, "Get out of that car." It was my mother standing on the porch with her head tied up and a long white gown. I got out of the car and he took off like a bat out of hell. "Why did you do that?" I asked her crying. "I told you when you get home don't be setting out there in no car, you get out of there and get in this house." She was still screaming. I sat on the porch the rest of the night. I was embarrassed and humiliated. This was the nicest guy I had ever been out with. I was so angry with my mother. She didn't come to my rescue when I needed her and there were many times when I needed her. The remaining of the summer was long.

I was off to find work that this high school diploma was supposed to get me. My first visit to the employment office and I was so excited. There were others there who had graduated with me. They called my name, "Shirley Jean Sims." "Good luck," said the lady I had been sitting next to. "Thank you," I said. I was feeling kinda sorrow for her because she didn't have a diploma. "Here's my diploma," I was saying as I reached it to the white lady. She never looked up, "I don't need to see that," She said. "I got this job for you at Bells Laundry they need somebody for today, one of the worker laid out musta stayed out too late last night. We give ya'll these jobs and you don't appreciate them. Here take this slip with you, next." "Ain't this a bitch," I said, "You white folk's sumpin else." I could have been a high school drop out for all she cared.

I walked the ten blocks to get there without a chance to rest. I was put to work immediately. I worked there until six that evening. He paid me two (2) dollars out of his pocket. "I'll call you if I need you." And with that he dismissed me. I knew he wouldn't call me. We didn't have a telephone and he didn't asked for my number. "This white man is some kinda stupid, I thought, if he thinks I'll be coming back. I've got my diploma and Miss Barksdale said this was gonna get me a good job." I was saying as I walked home.

This made me even more determined to go to college. I had graduated with so much anticipation for my future. This experience was the beginning of many similar ones. I knew that white men looked at us as a piece of tail. They kill you if they thought you would complain, and loved it when you resisted.

I had an after school job in the mill hill where the poor whites lived. They were workers at the Arkwright Mill and lived in the houses that the mill owned. I worked two afternoons a week for four dollars. I had to vacuum her rooms, hang her husbands' work clothes on the line and clean up the kitchen after they finish eating. She always fixed them a steak and the trimmings. When they finished she would offer me what was left on her plate. "Shirley I left some steak on my plate that you can have." She would say. "Yes mam." I would say but be thinking "If she think I'm gonna eat after her she's crazier than she looks, I wouldn't feed it to my dog if I had one." She and her husband talked about things and black folks as if I wasn't around. "What grade did you go to Shirley," she asked me. "I'm a senior in high school," I said with a lot of pride. "Oh, I didn't know you were still in school, if you don't have any plans you can start working for us full time." "No Madam, I'm going to college." "How you gonna do that, ya'll got money." She sneered. "No Madam, I got scholarships. I'm going to become a medical doctor." I said.

She was finished with this conversation. She called her husband to take me home. I always got in the back seat and remained silent all the way home but this night I decided to get in the front seat. I showed them I wasn't that "dumb nigger" they thought I was. As soon as we got out of the drive way and he straighten up the car to go forward his hands were up my dress and up and down my legs. I stiffen up and rode silently home with his hands still under my dress. I got out of his car and ran all the way home crying. I didn't go in for quite some time because I *was too upset and I didn't want my momma to see me. I knew she would fuss. I shouldn't been up there in that front seat in the first place. I never went back to that job. It had served its purpose. I was working to save money to pay my class dues so I could go to the Junior Senior Prom. I had made enough to do that. I never told this.*

"Shirley, you stay with Sadie. Because she don't need to be by herself, we've decided," my mother was telling me. No one asked me if I wanted to. No one ever ask me what I wanted, they always told me. I murmured as I walked away to get some clothes to live with Aunt Sadie. I learned Aunt Sadie wasn't as sick as everyone thought, it was her way of swindling the insurance company. She was sick by day and entertainer by night. This lady was a monster. It was worst been here than it was at home with Ben, and all them children.

"Oh he just like you baby, you'll be alright," Aunt Sadie was saying to me. I was trying to tell her how Lonnie C had raped me while she was gone. She had left on the pretense that she needed to borrow some drinks for the store from the lady up the street. No sooner than she left he started in on me. I fought until I had no more strength and I just gave in. I was whimpering when she came back. I wanted to crawl in a hole and die. They fixed themselves a drink and went on as if everything was normal. Where do I go, who do I turn to? I went home the next day and tried to tell my mother that I wanted to come home but she said Sadie needed me.

This became an every night thing until I left for school. I was so afraid that I would become pregnant again and not be able to go to school. Lonnie C bragged that he had the old woman and me. I was no longer the goody good girl; I was just like my grandma and Fannie Mae said, "I was going to' grow up to be nothing."

Albert was two years old and Angela was two weeks old when I went away to college Ricky was born my sophomore year at Livingstone College. Everyone in my dorm was excited about my new brother. They named him. He was two weeks old when I saw him for the first time. Well we finally got one that looks like the Jones I thought, he looks just like Southern, my mama's brother. He looked as if he was two months old instead of two weeks. He was the biggest baby I'd ever seen. Although I had two years of college and had lost my bed, I went on automatic and began to take care of him just as I had done with all of the others. Two weeks later her first grandchild, Ronnie Carl was born, June 12th 1961. I was nineteen, Mary Alice was seventeen and Helen was thirty-five.

Angela was a toddler about two and a half years old and Albert about four. These last three was almost like starting a new family. Sandra was almost five before any more babies came and this time after Ricky, Dr. Pettis did not wait on Ben's permission to tie Helen tubes.

Mary Alice began working at the hospital after school, she met and became engaged to Roland Goss. Helen couldn't win the argument about her being too young, "what about you, you wasn't but fifteen when you had Shirley," she would throw back in her defense. "Yes Mary Alice I don't want you to make the same mistake," Helen would argue back with her. Mary Alice always stood up to her and would talk back, not me, I was too afraid of a whopping, Mary Alice said, "a whopping didn't mean nothing to her but to change her tactics." She wanted out of this situation as much as I did and "saw no money for her to go to college because Helen was sending it all to you," she told me recently. Marrying Roland was going to be her escape but his mother changed all of that.

"We only had unprotected sex that one time and I got pregnant with Ronnie. I know now why his mother wouldn't own her grandchild. Her husband was gone and Roland was the oldest. She needed his help more than a grandchild." There's a soft side of Mary Alice I've seen many times when it's just she and I. When our uncle Ed died and all of the family were home for his funeral she showed the soft side. "I like that dress you've got on," she said. "Thanks, I made this to wear for my wedding to Johnnie, I said. "You know I'd like to get married someday," she said with loneliness in her voice. I wanted to reach out and hug her and tell her everything would be all right. I hesitated. Hugging is something we don't do.
"Everybody needs somebody, I said as we joined the march. Later in the presence of others, I said, "Since you like this dress so much I will give it to you to wear at your wedding."
"What the hell make you think I'm going to marry anyone, and I don't want your damn dress," she said angrily/sarcastic defending her security wall she had built around her.

She had suffered much hurt and had to bear it the best she knew how. I remember the long week her husband, J C, laid corpse. They had only been married a few months when they received their first income tax check and was able to catch up on bills and had a few dollars left. They'd decided to go out to Topsy's café together and have a little fun. She was going to get one of the girls to come stay with Ronnie and Sue and she was going to pay them. J C left the house and told her he'd be back to pick her up in about an hour and she'd ought to be ready by that time. She got busy making the arrangements and getting dressed. She hadn't had a night out in a long time and she missed those weekends at Topsy. She was getting a little restless when someone ran up on her porch yelling, "J C's been shot."

Grief is a strange emotion because it comes in so many forms. Grief is a portion of every emotion that God created. Psychologist says there are steps you go through but they cannot tell you how you will react to each emotion or each step. I remember Mary Alice wouldn't go to the burial because she didn't want to witness his "being put into the ground"; it was too final. After the funeral comes the returning of the family to the home to be greeted by the many friends and neighbors to feast and fellowship. Monday morning everyone has returned to their appointed place and the grief sets in.

When Johnnie died all I could think about were how tired I was and the big relief that it's all over, and sudden guilt that you feel relief and not sorrow. In the six months of Johnnie's illness I took care of him twenty-four seven and knew he was dying. We had a chance to make it right but J C was nineteen, full of life and ready to embark the responsibility of husband and father for Ronnie and Sue and soon another one. His death was a hard blow for Mary Alice, then the loss of her twins, and two little girls, both lived for only six weeks. "God don't put no more on you than you Can carry" is a common saying I've heard ever since a child. Is this scripture or is this myth? I think it a myth we use as an excuse to justify the choices in life we make.

I had too much to do at school to be trying to settle problems at home with my siblings and Helen. I was now a college student and this was my escape from poverty and ignorance and I can't let her or anyone else take this from me. It's my chance to be "somebody" and not "nothing" like Miss Geneva said. I had survived Miss Spradley and Molucy and was now on campus feeling like a college student. I was so excited about all of the new things to learn and embarrassed of the many things I didn't know about. How to fix my hair, or wear makeup, or shaving your legs, or wearing tampons.

I needed to find me a summer job so that I'd be ready to return to school in the fall. I had hoped to go to New York and get me one of those $1.25 an hour jobs but that didn't happen. It's Fourth of July and everyone went celebrating except the two babies and me. I sat on the front poach rocking the babies to quieting them down hoping they would fall asleep, one did and the other one didn't. How do I do this and out of frustration I began to cry, "why am I here with these two babies instead of celebrating like everyone else?" when Ma, my grandmother, came to my rescue.

When Helen came home Ma laid her tongue on her and Mary Alice for leaving those babies with me. I was again washing diapers out of water they'd soaked in all week, washing them and all of the other dirty clothes in the old wringer washer on the back poach. I don't remember where we got the machine from but we still had to draw and carry the water to the washing machine on the back poach and that was an afternoon of work. Helen was still sewing for the public and having problems with Mary Alice.

She put us, Mary Alice and I on a restricted curfew, leave before nine, leave together and return together, and be in by eleven. That was fine for Mary Alice but I was almost twenty, a sophomore in college, raising her "chillums" and she all of a sudden playing mama; I challenged her rules all summer. I only wanted to go out on Monday's and Thursday nights to the VFW because they had live music on those nights and the band didn't start playing until ten o'clock. I would go out without Mary Alice who had very different friends from me and very different interest from me. She was busy with the boys and I was interested in the music and being in the presence of older matured people like my friends in college.

"It was after two O' Clock when you came in here this morning," she would say up in my face. "Yea I know, I've told you the band doesn't start playing until ten and plays until two. I come home after the band stops playing, I've said this a hundred times, I don't understand why you don't trust me and why am I being punished because of Mary Alice's actions. I am a young adult Helen and it's time you start treating me like one," I said as I walked to the kitchen to wash the dishes that weren't washed after dinner last night and fill the empty water buckets for cooking and drinking. "Well I guess you know you won't be going anywhere for the next two weeks," she said belting out her punishment.
"O K," was all she got out of me. I knew the routine. I'd stay home for two weeks and go and stay again until after the band finished playing.

Dancing was still a favored pass time for me. I'd dance for as long as the band played with or without a partner. Guys lined up to dance with that "little Sims girl" with them big legs from Arkwright. It was a time when eyes were on me instead of my eyes being on a bunch of babies. Dancing was all that I was interested in but there were some who wanted more and some who tried to make it more.

I was afraid of these city boys and I didn't trust them. They were only interested in having sex and acted as if they were God's gift to women, they didn't even have a conversation. I had one to walk up and put a nut that you use to tighten screws in my hand, although this had never been done to me I knew what it meant. This boy later made time for raping his twelve-year-old sister and impregnating her. When I was in the tenth grade I went on the tenth graders field trip to Bethune Cookman's College in Daytona Beach, Florida. I worked an afternoon job to pay for this trip. We were all in the swimming pool and I was off to myself when Gerald Bobo swam over to me and grabbed me around my waist and stuck his fingers up my vagina while still holding onto me. When he let me go I had to leave the water because I was in so much pain. I was embarrassed that he would do that to me and I thought I liked him. He spoiled the remaining of my trip. I knew he had told the other boys what he had done to me. I wanted to tell Mr. Lyles and Mrs. Phillips but I was afraid of what they would do to me. I didn't know why I was afraid to tell. The subconscious mind knew why I was afraid and unconsciously I knew not to tell.

My attitude toward Ben changed when I went away to college; I wasn't afraid of him anymore. He was just a little old pussycat mama's boy who never grew up and thought he was to have his way. Aunt Della says, "he was Papa's first grandchild and Papa spoiled him. He's had a car ever since he was a teenager." They were almost the same age as was Aunt Sallie and Uncle Leonard close in age to his other brothers. "But there was nothing like Bennie as far as Papa was concerned, Aunt Della continued, it was that car that caused him not to graduate and he only had a few months to graduate. Driving that car, drinking, and running around with women is your daddy honey, that's all he knows to do."

When he took me to college along with his mother, Miss Geneva and Dot Wilkie, Helen's friend, he charged me. I had to put gas in his car and pay him out of the thirty-five dollars I had saved from odds and ends jobs. I think I saw him for who he was for the first time. He really wasn't my daddy, he may have supplied the seed that made me, but that was where the buck stopped. Helen couldn't come because Angela was only two weeks old; the older women said you couldn't come out of the house until the baby is a month old. I made five to six stops during this one hundred and twelve mile trip for him to get a beer and for him to pee. Miss Geneva talked the entire trip about how fast I was and what they wasn't "gonna" put up with from me. I tuned her out as I had learned to do early in life with Helen, Ben, and her. Daddies are supposed to protect their little girls not use them and abuse them. It was at that moment that I realized that I despised him and Miss Geneva too.

I am home for the summer of my sophomore year and I haven't felt this good about myself in years. College was just what I needed. I had returned with a new attitude about my future because I knew without a doubt that I was going to be successful. I had worked in the Library during the school year dusting flowers and book shelves. I never checked out a book that year I'd just pick me one from the shelf, read it and return it to its space. I had learned how to speak properly and not say fore but four and ax but ask, I knew how to fix my hair and didn't need Mary Alice to burn me anymore.

Fannie Mae, my daddy's sister, once straighten my wet hair. It was Easter Sunday and she had worked all day Saturday at the shop and now "here Helen is with all of dem little nappy head chillums." When it was my turn my hair had dried where I couldn't comb it. I wet my hair so I could comb it. I was nine years old. "I'll teach you not to wet this nappy head again," she said as she put that hot straighten comb next to my scalp. You could hear the sizzling sound made when the hot comb touched the wet hair making steam that burned the scalp. I screamed from the pain. "Shut-up, you had no business wetting your hair and you gonna sit here till I finish," she said with her voice trembling as it did so many time when she'd speak to me.

I couldn't stand to be outside in the sun for three or four days because the sun burned my scalp. I hated Easter. There were always arguments on Monday after Easter about me being dressed better than Mary Alice and they had to buy her something decent. I never understood this argument. We'd always have on the same outfits as a matter of fact Mary Alice looked the best. She was a cute little plump girl whereas I was the skinny one with the nappy hair.

I had come home for a weekend from school and Helen said my hair needed fixing and told Mary Alice to "fix it". She had taken cosmetology in school and learned to "fix hair". She would play in the food Helen would fix for me to take back to school, cake, and other snack foods. Once she cut a big block of cake out of the middle and put an emptied Ritz crackers box in my box Helen had packed for me. She didn't want to do my hair and made sure that I would never ask her to do it again. She put the straighten comb on my scalp to burn each time she put it in my hair. After a couple of these burns I got up and finished my own hair; and she was right; I've never asked her to do anything for me since.

I never recognized jealousy as the cause of our strained relationship as sisters. I always envied her with all of the attention she got. I saw her as the prettiest and the smartest because that's what I always heard said about her. I'd wish I'd had what she had so everybody would love me like they loved her. My brother Poochie once said, "Mary Alice should d' been the oldest because you ain't got sense enough to be the oldest." Whoa you gotta have sense to be the oldest, I thought, she can be the oldest she looks it. I wouldn't say it to her because I didn't want to hurt her feelings and make her dislike me even more.

When she got pregnant the first time Miss Geneva came and offered to take the baby and raise it so Mary Alice's life wouldn't be "messed up". I remember the summer Uncle Sam took her to New York and left me crying. I wanted to be with Uncle Sam more than anything. Dot Walker had told me he was my daddy. I wanted to believe that because he was such a handsome man and always came home in the biggest car. He'd pass out dollars to all of us standing around and give Mary Alice a five-dollar bill while grabbing her up in a swing and telling her how beautiful she was. Everywhere he went she went but I couldn't go. I was either in the way or needing to sit down.
"Git outa the way gurl or sit down somewhere gurl, or go outside and git outa grown folks mouth, gurl," where frequent orders from Ben and everybody else in the house including Mary Alice and Jackie Boy. Everybody told Shirley what to do and still tries to tell Shirley what to do.

I fail to understand why others become wrapped up in others affairs and neglect their own affairs. I never figured out why Helen thought I would be able to help her solve her problem with Mary Alice when she and I had a problem that hadn't been resolved. Mary Alice was pregnant again, Suzette, June 29th, 1962, this time with a different boy, J. C. Teamer. I am now a married woman after getting pregnant by Joe Bynum Tugman, the father of all of my children and Helen's still making phone calls about Mary Alice.

"She and J.C. gonna get married on mother's day and we'll have our mothers' day dinner and a wedding the same day," my mother was saying. We had started celebrating her mama and daddy's wedding anniversary on mother's day and this was going to be their fiftieths year of marriage.

"Ok Helen, I'll be there on Saturday so I can help with the dinner and the arrangements, have they gotten their license yet?" I asked. "No not yet but they go git them," she said with a little doubt in her voice. "I'll see you Saturday Helen, bye," I said hanging up. Well this should solve her problems with Mary Alice now that she's getting married she'll no longer be her responsibility. Joe and I got there on Saturday afternoon and they had not gotten the marriage license. "If they didn't get them yesterday Helen he didn't mean to get them because government offices are closed on Saturday so what's going on," I asked "I don't know what they gonna do, Earline called and she all upset that J. C. changed his mind. She said that he just wasn't ready," she said with a sad look on her face. "Well Helen it wasn't meant to be, they both are still so young, they aren't nothing but babies themselves," I said wondering how she was going to solve this problem now.

Mary Alice and J. C. eventually got married after Suzette was born and she was pregnant again, this time by J. C. again. I bet he didn't stand a chance with his mother Miss Earline. "That girl you'd done got pregnant again, you going to marry her." Five months after their marriage he was killed by a sixteen year old neighbor behind "boys ruffling each other up." Estee's brother had been found murdered after being missing for two weeks and when he ran home to tell his daddy about the older boys picking on him his daddy gave him the gun to go back and, " take up for yourself, they picked up one of mine with a shovel they won't kill another." This was brought out in testimony in court.

Mary Alice miscarried the twins she was pregnant with by her nineteen- year old husband and she was a widow at eighteen with two small babies, Ronnie two and Suzette one. I took Suzette back to Salisbury with me after staying two weeks after the funeral. I needed to get back home and try to find me a teaching position. I had tried to find a position in or around Salisbury. My marriage was too shaky to work out of town. Joe refused to move. The only job available to me was in Morehead City, NC, Kings High School. I taught eight through the twelfth with the population of the school a little less than three hundred students with eleven seniors.

Helen began to call me about the problems she was having with "Poochie" not going to school. Miss Littlejohn, the school secretary gave Helen Poochie' report card at a PTA meeting and she learned about all of his absentees. Poochie uses to get on the bus at one stop and off at the next stop. I would beg him to go to school and he would say with his little defiant face, "you go to school if you want somebody to go to school, I bet I'll make more money than you'll make, so leave me along."

I came to Spartanburg and took Poochie back to Salisbury with me, put him in school and solved that problem. He made grades good enough to pass the ninth to the tenth and was very proud and ready to return back to school now that Pat won't be a grade ahead of him but they would be in the same grade. He could take that better than her being a grade ahead of him. Mr.

Woodson wouldn't wait for his transfer papers to come from Price High School in Salisbury to prove he had been in school that year and put him back in the ninth grade. He wouldn't wait until I straighten it out and quit going.

That was the end of his school days and the beginning of his full time hustling career. He was the biggest dope pusher in the area. He took ownership of the Arkwright community for selling dope. No one else could stand up against him. Once when he heard that I was selling marijuana he set up his selling business on a stump in front of my house and built an extra room onto the "Mug Club" to take my poker games I was having. It didn't matter that the beer license for the Mug Club were in my name, it was always about him, he would take them off the wall on Sunday and be wide opened for business selling beer and liquor and dope in the building. So what if they were in my name? That didn't jeopardize him and he was all he ever thought about. What if there had to be a choice between him and me. I can't blame him for the way he acted because he didn't have an image of a father or a husband to pattern after. He always saw Helen handling things such as grocers, lights and whatever else needed to be taken care off and that's the way he believed things were to be. Ben always put his little bit of money on the dresser for Helen to buy grocers and that was the extent of his financial contribution.

When Helen gave him the responsibility of paying the light bill the lights were turned off every month and always stayed two months behind. He always had a car and had to make payments on that and a bill at a service station to keep gas in it. Helen was using money from Ronnie and Sue's social security checks to pay the light bill and help make out the house payment. Ben became so cruel to them that Mary Alice had to come get them. She had moved to New York and was trying to be established as an LPN and needed time away from her children to do this. She had gone through so much tragic in her short life besides losing her husband at seventeen. After the miscarriage she married J. C.'s best friend "Bug Eye," I was teaching in Morehead City, NC when I got the phone call.
"Shirley, Mary Alice just walked through here and announced that she's marrying "Bug Eye," she was saying with disgust in her voice, he's so ugly with that big o jaw. I wonder what's in his jaw." "Helen, I said, stopping her in the middle of her criticism, did you ask her why and what's going on? "No, I d' n ax her nothing. I just said for what, and she just walked out," trying to defend herself. "Tell Mary Alice to call me and let me know if she needs me," I said as I hung up the phone.

I was more upset with Helen than I was with Mary Alice. I knew she was still mourning the death of her husband and Bug Eye was the closest thing to him. That's why she clanged to him trying to make sense out of her young life and having no place to turn, she turned to him. J C had been dead only nine months when she married Bug Eye and became pregnant with their little girl "Peanut." I never got to see her before she died at six weeks of crib death nor her other little girl that died at six weeks. Dr. Pettis said, had she lived she would have been severely retarded. Her death was a blessing and a miracle for Mary Alice who had not yet passed twenty. Her destiny was beginning to look identical to Helen's. She recognized same as I did that she had to get the hell out of Spartanburg to turn her life around.

Poochie never left home and he should have. He died a lonely man at the age of forty-four of colon cancer. The mother of his two girls had married someone else, and his wife Ann and their daughter Francine, had moved on. She was Ann's daughter but Poochie accepted her as his and she called him daddy. It was members of our family that did not accept Ann or Francine. They lived in the house with Ben and Helen when they first married with Albert moving out of his room; it became Poochie and Ann's room. Neither Helen nor the girls respected Ann. They wouldn't eat her cooking and talked about it within her hearing. Helen allowed the door from the living room to the hall to be paneled up so they had no privacy; you had no other choice but to go through their room. Poochie probably thought this was the thing to do because this is how Ben had done when he married Helen, moved in with his mama.

They left and moved in with her mother and soon in Spartan Terrace, which was brand new at that time. Ann had attended South Carolina State for a couple of years when she became pregnant with Francine. I don't know how she and Poochie met and don't remember their courtship because I was married and living in Salisbury, NC. It was a strange relationship to me because they had nothing in common, she being a college student and him a high school dropout. She always had a job and he always hustled by selling dope and cutting card tables. The marriage lasted about two years with her leaving him not being able to cope with his lifestyle and the jeopardy he was putting her in with her job. She worked for Southern Bell and had worked herself up to a supervisory position and could not afford to have the reputation of her husband destroy her career. This was devastating to Poochie because he really loved Ann but only admitted it to me. The others were happy for the breakup, now they got their brother back and can pick up where they left off before she came into the picture.

After she left he would call me and talk for hours, he didn't want to talk to any of the others, he said, "Because I don't want to hear nothing bad said about Ann." "It's like I've always told you Poochie, you can stop that and you need to stop it, you need to get them girls out of your business," I said as I had said many times about his relationship with his sisters and his wife. They don't have to like her but they do have to respect her as your wife.

He moved in with me, for I had left Joe and was now living in Spartanburg once again. He continued to sell dope while living in my home with my three boys and me, again thinking only of himself. He moved into my house and never gave me a dime the whole time he lived with me. I gave him Scooter's room, my oldest son, had a telephone put in, and fixed it up to accommodate him. He was more comfortable than he had ever been. It was a new home I had bought when I first came to Spartanburg after leaving Joe. Joe was a wife beater along with a few other things and was still bothering me, taking the boys, breaking into my home and stealing important papers and threatening me. I was glad to have him with me plus I thought he would help me out with the mortgage and grocers but that didn't happen. He would have his women to stay overnight and wallow around in my house as if it was his. I became the intruder on his privacy. I would come home from work and someone would be in the kitchen cooking for him and my boys would be outside or all back in one room.

Needless to say I was glad when he moved into the trailer left by Uncle Albert's wife after he died and she returned to Pittsburg where her children were. Uncle Albert and Uncle Jonas were Miss Geneva's brothers that moved to Pittsburg as young men to work in the steel mills. There was plenty of work for a Black Man in Pittsburg and no work but farm work or sharecropping in South Carolina. They had done that all of their lives until they saved enough to catch a train to Pittsburg. *They would come home during the summers in their big cars and their high yellow women. Uncle Jonas wife looked "white" and he and Uncle Albert were as black as they come. The two used to argue which one was the blackest. Uncle Jonas would cry because Uncle Albert would always win the argument. They had said that they would return home to live when they retired. That's why Uncle Albert was here, he had retired at sixty-five after many years at the steel mill. He had gone hunting in Asheville with some friends and had a massive heart attack returning back to the car where they had parked. He had been home less than six months since he retired and Aunt Elsie was too heartbroken to stay here away from her family and children. She left the trailer they had purchased and Poochie took over the payments.*

Glenda Patricia, what a pretty name and I picked it all by myself, we call her Pat. I thought the name sounded sophisticated and important and would take her a long ways. She was twenty months old when Joyce Elaine was born. Pat never had her due time, she was the "Black" one that looked like them Jones's. The Ducketts were the blackest people I knew besides Beaufort Keenon. Miss Geneva didn't take to her; her hair was short thick and nappy. She used to stand next to Helen's taffeta yellow curtains in the sitting room and rub them between her fingers and suck on her thumb until she'd fall asleep. Pat and Lane were my assignment and Jackie and Sandra were Mary Alice's assignment. We had to iron their clothes and braid their hair and get them ready for school, church or wherever we had to go.

I heard about the fight she and Ben had because he called her "black." I wasn't there I was still living in Salisbury and teaching school in Edgefield, South Carolina. She was just as sensitive to being called "Black" as I was being called "red." I had just bought my first car, brand new, a 1964 Malibu Chevrolet, white with an aqua top. I stopped in to see what was the problem and stayed overnight with the intentions of going on to Salisbury the next morning. I knew Joe would be upset because he looked forward to my coming home so he can drive the car the whole weekend and this was shorten him a day. Pat drove my car to take Helen grocery shopping. She was tired waiting on Ben and ordered, "Come on Pat and take me to the store." I was standing there, why not ask me, after all it was my car. I just stood there without a word. They were gone most of the morning. When they got back Pat had had an accident in my new car. "Some lady ran into the side of her and it wasn't her fault," Helen said, don't worry about it, ain't you got insurance?" I left without addressing the problem. I knew there will be trouble when I get to Salisbury and Joe sees this bent door on the passenger's side. I had bought this car in June 1964 and this was September, only three months old. All they had to say was "don't worry."

The nine months I worked in Morehead City I rode the bus home once a month. I would catch the 5:30 pm bus and get to Salisbury 7:30 am the next morning and return to a 7:30 pm bus and get to Morehead city about eight o'clock and go directly to school from the bus stop. During the school year I had taught the adults at night at the school for Carteret County Technical School and they owed me for the quarter. When they sent my money I bought me a car and drove to Spartanburg and bought Ben and Helen's house out of foreclosure. I returned to Salisbury to find the furniture truck backed up to my apartment about to empty my house. Joe had not made any of the payments I'd sent every month. I sent money for the rent, insurance, and furniture and he'd gambled the money just like he did the money I sent to buy some land. I had to wire him that hundred dollars so "Gerock," the local white grocery store owner in the "black" neighborhood," wouldn't get it."

I was slapped around pretty good for questioning that move. Joe cursed for a while and left speeding off in anger. He didn't return until Sunday evening for me to return to school; I didn't stop on my way back because it was getting late. The roads were long, dark and unfriendly. It was the sixties. "Black women" didn't need to be driving a new car with North Carolina Tags in South Carolina by herself. I would drive in the middle of the road until I'd meet a car not letting anyone pass me for fear they would stop me.

When Miss Geneva learned I had a car she had a fit, she let me know that Joe should be the one with that car. My "running up and down the highway." She said, "These people you think is your friends ain't your friends and soon you'll be getting a divorce and it'll be all your fault." I had decided to stop in and say hello on my way home. When she saw my car crossing the railroad tracks she began getting out of her chair and was in the street waiting for me to stop. She didn't give me the chance to speak before she jumped in my case about giving this car to Joe. She thought the sun rose and set on Joe because he'd always compliment her and Fannie Mae on how good and young they looked. They would just lap this up. The next time I saw her she was in the hospital dying from cancer. I leaned over and kissed her. I told her that I loved her. It was the first time I ever touched her or she touched me. The next time I saw her was at her funeral when I was pregnant with my second son, Chante' Lamont Tugman. I rode down on the train from Salisbury to Spartanburg.

In the meantime I kept my car and resigned from Kings High school in Edgefield, SC after I discovered I was pregnant with my first son, Joe Bynum, Jr. It had happened the weekend of Labor Day. We had been in school about two weeks and had our first holiday. I felt so important teaching school and being with my peers where I didn't have to apologize for being intelligent. I was sharing Miss Counts' home with another teacher, Miss Brown from Macon, GA. Miss Counts was the home economics teacher. She was well respected by both Black and Whites although the "whites didn't call her Miss.

I left Edgefield for Salisbury to spend the holiday with Joe, my husband with the excitement of being Mrs. Tugman the "swinging schoolteacher," the name the students gave me. Joe had other plans that didn't include me; he was anxiously waiting for the car stating that I had made him late. I was disappointed that he didn't have time for me. I'd been gone for two weeks. He left without even a hug or a kiss, just a, "I'll see you later," as he was taking the car keys from my hand. He returned the next morning broke, tired, and mean as a hornet. I began to try to cuddle up and tell him how I'd missed him when he shoved me so hard I fell from the bed. I began to cry and ask why he was so mean to me when he grabbed me and pulled me back into the bed and raped me. "Now, are you satisfied?" he asked as he turned over and went to sleep. I missed my October period. Joe was borne June 20th 1965 on Father's day.

September of 1965 I had a three-month-old baby. A teaching job at Garnard High School in Gaffney, SC. I had planned to stay with Mary Alice but moved in with Helen. She moved in shortly after I did. We were all back home again this time, her bringing Ronnie and Suzette and *me with my son, Joe/Scooter. We all stayed in the one bedroom with two double beds. I don't know how we did it but we did.*

I worked by day and Poochie drove my car by night. It became a family car instead of my car. Everyone with licenses drove my car; it was wrecked seven times in seven years. It was a completely different car from what I bought. Every body part had been replaced because of the wrecks. I returned to Salisbury at the end of the school year without signing my contract for renewal. My marriage was shakier than when I was in Morehead City, NC. Joe's constant accusations were getting fierce. I was becoming more frightening of him, not only for my safety but Scooter's also. Joe was actually jealous of my relationship with my son. He was all I had that loved me unconditionally and still does.

I was back in Salisbury again trying to savage my marriage that got even worst. Now I am out of work. When I am out of work, my family suffers. Joes' habits came before Scooter and me. Payday for him meant money to pay for his weekly drawing of "ball tickets," have his car cleaned, a bottle of J&B Scotch, a carton of Pall Mall cigarette, and off to the "Hut" to gamble the remaining of the night. He would return the next day in time to get to work without a dime in his pocket. Nothing was bought for the house including food and no one was paid, including rent.

This was his routine from the very beginning of our marriage. He brought me home on our wedding night and asked, "Could you let me have a few dollars until Wednesday payday?" "Sure," I said without hesitation. I got my purse. He was right there looking over my shoulders, "Give me that twenty," he said smiling at the little money I had in my purse. It was only a hundred dollars I had saved from my job in New York that summer. It was to pay toward my tuition that was $300.00. Wednesday payday he had "borrowed" the entire $100.00. School would be starting in just a few weeks. I would be four months pregnant and able to finish the first semester. The baby was due February. I had to graduate.

I cried on my wedding night. This is not how it was supposed to be. I was supposed to be sleeping in the arms of my husband with him telling me how blessed he was to have me. Instead he had brought me home, "made love" to me, got up, dressed, asked for money, and returned home about six o'clock am Monday morning August 13, 1962. Tthe first might of my marriage to Joe B. Tugman.

Joyce Elaine was twelve and Jackie was ten, Sandra was nine, Albert was five, Angela was three and Ricky and Ronnie were fifthteen months old. All were so young and so vulnerable, I wanted to take them all with me. Sandra was the most demanding. She had been the baby almost as long as I had been an only child. I taught her to say mama and daddy, none of us before Sandra said mama and none but her say daddy. I stopped teaching the others to say daddy when he asked me, "What the hell was I calling him daddy for?"

Sandra awoke one morning with her face twisted from "Bell Palsy," it was the strangest thing to happen to a child, I thought. "Did you take her to the doctor yet, Helen, I asked. "Not yet, I was thinking it might go back if I rubbed something on it," she said apologetically. "Get her to a doctor and I'll be down there this weekend unless you need me earlier. It was never determined what caused this to happen to a child. Then Joyce developed Rheumatic Fever following a bout with Strep throat. She was in the fourth grade. Jackie's eyesight was so bad her glasses were being changed every year and getting thicker and thicker. Helen had a bad cold the entire time she was pregnant with Jackie; all of those home remedies is what probably affected her eyesight; she's blessed she's not blind.

Albert was sort of thrown to the side because Ben only fooled with whoever the baby was and that was Ricky. He would leave five year old Albert standing on the porch crying wanting to go while taking Ricky. Albert didn't have the time with him that Poochie and Ricky had and didn't develop the hustling skills they did from Ben. Helen always said, "Poochie was the kind of gangster Ben wanted to be but he had too many children."

These girls were back to back in school. Just a grade or two difference and all in at the same time. Mary Alice and I had finished with our schooling, Mary Alice from the school for practical nursing in Gaffney, SC and me graduating from Livingstone College, Salisbury, NC. Helen became active in the PTA and the girls became involved in after school activities, which was a plus. I never attended a high school basketball game and only went to a football game on homecoming day. Helen would drive them and pick them up from parties and to and from meetings or whatever they were involved in. I was happy for them experiencing things that I didn't experience. I hoped they would follow in Mary Alice's and my footsteps and get educated in something that was going to give them a decent job to escape poverty and ignorance and be professional as we were.

There wasn't much emphasis placed on education when I was coming along. The opportunities for Black Women were limited to teaching and nursing, if you came from the Dr. Douglas' or Dr. Bull's home. For the rest of us it was trying to get a job at some of the rich "white folks" houses. Poor "crackers" didn't have no more than you had. They couldn't pay a decent wage for the work they wanted done, plus they were nasty. They let their cats and dogs live inside their house. Their houses always smelled like dog or cat and wet stinky hair. I was determine that this was not going to be my destiny, I would go to New York or someplace where they needed sleep-in maids and paid $50.00 a week. I'd save my money and come back home a rich black woman and have me a maid.

You can imagine the excitement for the opportunity to go to college; it came to me through Mr. Clemons, a Livingstone graduate who paid for my SAT and suggested the colleges to send my scores. Livingstone College, South Carolina State, and Bennett College offered me scholarships and I accepted Livingstone College's offer.

I had always known knowledge of God was the key to success and the key to wealth. When reading the Word God's people were always victorious over their enemies. Poverty and ignorance are two of our greatest enemies. We never identify them because we have accepted it as a way of life. To be poor is to be holy is a philosophy believed by many, some sect vow poverty and the Baptist teaches how hard it is for a rich man to get into heaven than for a camel to go through the eye of the needle. Since you know that's an impossibility then the conclusion is if you get rich you'll go to hell. Off course we know that this is not what it means but it's a good ellipsis for anyone needing an excuse for being poor and ignorant. A house divided by itself will fall and this is what Satan has done through the family. Slavery, reconstruction, sharecropping, lynching, Jim Crow era, and integration destroyed our family structure, and the family, which is God's Church, is in a state of confusion.

Everything is in order and everything obeys except man.
You don't hear the same sounds during the day that you hear at night.
Yet they are the same sounds every day and every night.
Some nights and some mornings there's a sound that hadn't been heard.
Like a flock of birds taking off makes a whoosh sound.
They move on the demand of the hawk's gawk.
The Kildee announces here they come, diverts the nest.
The rabbit rustling the grass hiding the entrance to his underground tunnels.
The beaver building his dam that the subdivision destroyed.
The geese lining up for an easy feed on the algae and small fish.
The caterpillar crossing over to metamorphic with the colors of a queen.
Nature knows when to plant, and when to harvest.
When to live and when to die.
When to stay and when to go.
When to grow and when to rest.
When to hibernate and when to mate.
When to lie and when to sit.
When to kill and when to yield.
Nature knows and obeys.
Nature is God.
What is man?   Shirley Sims Gray © 2005

When Pat was about ten and I was fifteen I came in and was going to use the water she had drawn for her bath to bathe the younger girls so I could finish my chores for the day. She stood her grounds about that being her water and I couldn't convince her differently, she even got physical with me. I knew from that that she would be a fighter and stand up for herself. I knew it was going to be tough standing up to the Sims side of the family, I never added up " enough" to ever get a "you did good," not once in my lifetime from any of them. Ma, Helen's mama, will say to me when I'd complaint about someone not liking me, "if they ain't giving you nothing to make you go to the closet then you don't worry about what they say, they just jealous anyhow."

I was never able to believe that anyone could be jealous of me, what did I have to be jealous off? I am the outside child that ain't gonna be nothing. Probably have a house full of babies just like her Mama, was all expected of me, so why should anyone be jealous of that. Pat became popular in school by making good grades and participating in extra-curriculum activities at Carver High School. She had some of the same teachers I had when I attended Carver. They knew she was one of Shirley Sims younger sisters. They were proud of me for breaking the cycle by graduating from high school and college.

She was Captain of the Cheering Squad and a member of a social club she and some of her peers organized, and off course Joyce' group had to do the same. She was a senior at Carver and attended the Junior Senior Prom at Garnard High School in Gaffney, SC where I was junior advisor and chaperone for the prom. I was so proud to have her there as my guest and she was proud to have me as her big sister. That "proud" got lost somewhere in the shuffles of life.

I don't know anything about my younger sisters dating because I wasn't around during that time, I do know that they all were dating guys that were popular city boys that I didn't trust. I had just cause, they were drug addicts and thugs. They had cars, hustled, and had money. My sister Sandra said, "Rubber wheels beat rubber heels." The young man that liked her rode a bike to see her. When Kenneth Smith came along with his blue Mustang the little Tanner boy didn't have a chance. Pat was lucky she didn't marry her high school sweetheart, not so for Joyce and Sandra. Jackie didn't marry him or he wouldn't marry her. She stayed with him through a son and many years of him coming in and out of her life. Glenda Patricia went to Winston Salem State College, Winston Salem, NC and Joyce at South Carolina State, Orangeburg, SC, at the same time, Pat was a sophomore and Joyce a freshman.

Joyce Elaine was a child spoiled by Miss Geneva and Fannie Mae. She was a true Sims having a close resemblance to Fannie Mae and ways like them. They had her believing she was better than the rest of us. Dr. Pettis had diagnosed her with rheumatic fever when she was eight years old. She was home schooled by the teacher sending her homework. Our brother "Poochie" would correct it and sometimes do it over, "I wasn't gonna be passing in all of that wrong homework," he used to say.

Miss Geneva didn't think that Helen was capable of taking care of her as they could. Helen let them keep her most of the time, it gave her a break because she still had three little ones younger than her and was pregnant with Angela, baby number nine. I was a senior getting ready for graduation and college. Lane would boss them around and had them waiting on her hand and foot. "Bring me a drink of water," Miss Geneva or "I want this or I want that," was common orders. They catered to her every move. She thought everyone else should bow to her also. This is where she and Jackie Clashed. The two slept in the same room, no other choice, and didn't speak for years. Jackie would beat up on her whenever she got tired of her mouth and she had a lot of that. She could say whatever she wanted to say to you but it's a different story if it's turned on her. She's just like the little Feisty dog that yelps loudly and runs at the drop of a hat.

Joyce majored in physical education after convincing Helen to get a second opinion about her health. Dr. Pettis would not sign off on the restrictions she had had her under throughout her school years. She could not take PE because it was strenuous on her heart is why Dr. Pettis would not sign off. The "white" doctor gave the ok although Dr. Pettis has treated her all of these years. She not only knew her history but was friends to our family and cared about her, can we say that for the "white" doctor? I found that attitude to be prevalent in the "Black" community concerning decisions, "if it's white it's right" rules. "I want to go to college, she said, but if I can't major in PE then I won't go. So off to college she went. Her high school sweetheart, Charles "Butch" Atchison, Jr., the rich boy went to A &T in Greensboro, NC. She had to miss a semester because there just wasn't any money available. She lived with me that semester. I got her a job as a receptionist for Clint Jones, the dentist and a friend of Joe's and mine.

I was accepted to the School of Cytology in Concord, NC, July 8, 1968; Lamont was six months old borne February 2nd 1968. Every Wednesday was the day I chose to go to the employment office looking for work after being unsuccessful at finding a teacher's position within commuting distant. My profile was professional but the assigned "white" counselor only offered me domestic jobs. Every Wednesday I went to the same counselor and every Wednesday she would get jobs to offer me for non- professionals. She tried humiliating me by offering me domestic jobs. "Can you cook?" She would ask me sometimes. "Yea ma'am, politely.
"Miss Jones in the hospital and her doctor said she could come home if she had somebody to cook for her," she would say with a smirk. "Well if Miss Jones finds a cook tell her to let me know, if she's a good cook I might want to use her sometime," I would say as if I had a million dollars. I didn't have a dollars but I had my dignity and wasn't going to allow her to take any of it from me.

One day she wasn't there. A young "white" male counselor offered me a position that had come through from the government as a result of the Affirmative Action. She must have died because she was old as crap. "I had a job come in here just yesterday and placed it in file thirteen. I didn't think anyone would come in this soon with the qualifications you have." He was saying as he sat down to give me the job description and the directions to get to the Cabarrus County Hospital, Concord, NC.

To my amazement it wasn't a job but a school of Cytology. This hospital was a teaching hospital with schools for Nurses, Medical Technologist, Radiologist, Histotechnologist and Cytotechnologist. These are professions I'd never heard of except for nursing and I majored in biology. I knew there was a school of medical technology at Charlotte Memorial in Charlotte, NC because I had tried to enroll in 1964. They said I didn't have enough hours in chemistry, I enrolled at A &T University graduate school taking organic chemistry to get the required hours. I had eight and they said I needed twelve. Four years later I learned of the school in Concord, NC. They were about to lose their federal funding. Persistence is one of my God-given virtues.

As a Cytotechnologist we screen and diagnose Pap smears for cancer and other venereal diseases. Rachel Lucky from Landis, NC and I were the first Blacks to be accepted in the school, I claim first because she didn't come until a few days later. I was pregnant with my third son Steven Irvin, borne August 30, 1069, and graduated July 11th, 1969. Joe was four and Lamont was eighteen months. We lived off the two hundred dollar a month stipend I received for the twelve months I was in school. I would get up at five o'clock am and hang clothes out on the line that I had washed the night before, cook breakfast for Joe and the boys, make sure there clothes were laid out, and the crock pot was cooking today's dinner. My school was five days a week, eight hours a day, twelve months and at least two hours a night to prepare for tomorrow. Determination was my catalyst or the knot to tie at the end of the rope. "She go to school all the time," was the complaint from Joe's family, they couldn't understand why I was not content and neither could I sometimes. I knew I couldn't stop striving to better my situation.

I was busy decorating for Christmas with much excitement. We got our stipend early so I had just the one- day to shop for Christmas for the boys. I'd hoped Joe would give me something from his Christmas bonus, but the boys at the "Hut" took it all at the poker table. I asked if he would take me out. I could get Edith, the girl across the street who babysat for me, to come over and stay with the boys. They were already asleep anticipating Santa clause. "Where I'm going women ain't got no business there," he said as he left the house. I went out alone. I drove over to the "Hut." They wouldn't allow me in although my husband was in there. I couldn't believe he would be so bold thinking that I wouldn't leave the house. I left and drove to my Sister-in-law's house. She and I went to Lexington, NC about sixteen miles from home, had a beer, listen to a few songs on the jukebox, got bored and came home.

The sitter was gone. Joe had returned home. The doors were locked and so were the windows. He ignored my knocks and my hollering for him to open the door. I managed to get the window opened in my son's room. As I climbed in he stood there waiting on me. "Where have you been, bitch? He growled as he slapped me across the face, answer me now." "I went to Lexington with Gloria," is all I got out before he knocked me down and drugged me down the hall to our bedroom. I came too from the chocking with him screaming, "Die motherfucker, die." This night I knew I was going to die because of the severity of the beating. I had a busted lip, broken front teeth and burns on my thigh, and cigarette burns on my leg. I couldn't move from the cigarette. I was pinned down in the platform rocker. The climax of the beating was being thrown in the bed and raped. I went to school that Monday bruised and no one said a word to me. No one asked what happened.

I had no one or nowhere to go. I had called my mother to come get me after one of the beatings. She and Ben came. I was packed and ready to go. It was a good time because Joe was at work. "I hope you don't think I going to take you out of this house and Joe's not here, its two sides to every story Shirley," said Helen. "They was probably drinking," Ben said. They took a seat and waited for Joe to get off work. He came in. They went to the bedroom, without me, stayed about fifteen minutes. "Yea, Helen, if Shirley wants to leave, we'll go to the court house tomorrow and get legal separation papers and I'll bring her home myself," Joe said. Ok Joe, we'll talk later, Helen said, as she and Ben left me. THEY LEFT ME. ("If you think you're going somewhere Monday, it'll be a black Monday. It'll be a day you'll never forget. Now you put them damn curtains back up to the windows, and unpack them bags and take your ass to bed," as he walked out, returning to his poker table).

I stayed but began planning a get-away as soon as I finished school. I missed my January period. I gave birth to the most beautiful son in all the whole wide world, Steven Irvin Tugman. I immediately dedicated him to God as I had promised if I didn't abort my baby. His daddy had insisted on me aborting my baby. He had his sisters over to tell me how it's done. "Make her drink some white liquor mixed with black draught, that'll make her abort," his sister Ruth said. Call the school and tell them you want be there tomorrow, he ordered. God in his mercy spared my baby and my life and I'll forever be thankful to him.

I relived this scene many times during my separation from Joe and my sons. It was the catalyst that kept me moving forward. I left Joe November 1974. It was the same year I was crowned Miss Alumni of Livingstone College. I rode on the queen's float and was crowned *during half-time at the Homecoming game. It was such an honor to represent the Salisbury Alumnus and be the center of attention and queen for a day. I certainly wasn't a queen in my household. We had moved from the apartment on Standish Street in Salisbury to a house in Hawkins Town. I was so proud of our three- bedroom two- bath ranch house in the country. I bought the corner lot and had it cleared for my first garden. The boys had plenty of running space, Laney had her own room and I'm working as a Cytotechnologist at Rowan Memorial Hospital, Salisbury, NC. All of this and something was still missing. I joined the local Baptist church and became director of the youth but that didn't satisfy the something within that was striving for more.*

I was recently asked if I could be anything I'd want to be what would it be? "A wife, I answered, yes a wife. I don't need to be CEO or famous or any of those things, just a wife. Not a mother, not a grandmother, not auntie. All of that is good, but I've never had the opportunity to be a wife like as in Proverb thirty-one. I want my husband to be as Abraham was to Sarah, her lord and I want to be his queen. I want to cater to his every need and he to mine. I want him to be my best friend, my lover, my soul mate, my provider and my protector. I haven't had that from either of my marriage. I don't want to be the strong woman any longer, bring back the chivalry."

Mrs. Delia, Joe's mother, rode the bus from Salisbury, NC to Compton, CA and back to pick up her granddaughter, Laney. Joe had fathered while station there in the United States Air Force in 1957-1959. She had been asked by Marie Harris, Laney's mother, if she wanted Laney. She had married. Her husband wasn't willing to take care of both of Joe's children, Laney and Toney. She was going to give the girls up for adoption. Mrs. Delia told her that she would take Laney who was eighteen months old. She was about sixty years old at the time. She wasn't able to handle a toddler of this age but with determination and constant nagging at Joe, she managed the best she could.

Laney was four years old when Joe and I married and eleven years old when she came on her own to live with Joe and I. She showed up at my door on a school day, Wednesday, and announced that she came to live with me. I received her with some hesitation because I knew Mrs. Delia's feelings about her staying with me. She was concerned about how I would treat Laney and never hesitated to ask, "How's you treating Laney, instead of how is Laney doing?"

Laney wasn't accustomed to being told what she could or could not do. This caused a conflict between her and me. Joe took no part in her discipline, or any other things a father is supposed to be for a daughter. I couldn't direct him because I had not experienced any kind of amiable relationship with my daddy. She was a little girl that needed directions and love that I wasn't able to give her because I didn't know how too. I was experienced at taking care of babies, washing and changing diapers, dressing them, feeding them; not a nourishing mother, and this is what this child needed. She was exposed to the constant arguments between Joe and her grandmother who she called Mama. She was confused as I had been as a child. Wondering why no one liked her and why was she causing so many problems. She was afraid of Joe. She still talks about that frightening experience of him opening the door to the heater with a roaring fire and threaten to stick her in it just to get her off his back about money. Hindsight gives me understanding why she measured your love for her with what you give her.

She and I had our problems from the very beginning. I said to her, " young lady if you want to stay with me you can but there won't be any, you get mad at me and run to grandma's or mad at grandma and run back to me. It's going to be here with me or be with Miss Delia, not the both of us." The first weekend her Aunt Ruth, Joe' sister came to pick her up. She was all packed and ready to leave when Ruth realized that I wasn't included with the planning. "Young lady, did you get Shirley's permission to stay with mama this weekend?" Ruth asked. "No," she answered. "Why didn't you?" Ruth asked. "She don't have to know everything I do, I can't even go outside unless I tell her," she said, looking at me smirking up her face. "Well, you can just get your little old self back in your room until you learn some respect, you have to ask Shirley and yes she needs to know when you are not in the house where you are," Ruth said. Finally, I got into the conversation. "It's okay Ruth, it's going to take some time for her to get used to me and my rules. You can go this weekend but here after she has to get my permission to go there for the weekend and also coming home after school. She didn't come home Wednesday and went down to grandma's. I was worried sick as to where she was and called Miss Delia to see if she were there and she was. It's ok let her go please," I was almost begging.

Ruth took her. She was gone for the entire weekend. This gave me the opportunity to be with my sons, Joe two and a half years old and Lamont a few months old. Laney's presence and her needs were overwhelming. It changed my life completely. I found myself dealing with a defiant angry little girl and two small children and soon another teenager, Claudia, Ruth's daughter.

Ruth died suddenly at age 45 from an aneurysm and left her husband Rippy, and three teenage girls, Claudia, 17, Julia 15, and Meme 14. She and Rippy had rented this old landmark in Salisbury, the home of Dr. Trent. He was President Emeritus of Livingstone College after serving as President for many years. Dr. Samuel Duncan was President at this time. I was to meet her there the afternoon after getting out of school to measure for curtains. We planned this as we bowled together the night before. I was close to Elizabeth (Lib) and Ruth, Joe's two sisters that was older than he. We bowled together often. So did Joe and I, as a matter of fact, we were pretty good bowling in two leagues a week. We had all sorts of trophies. These were some of the good times with Joe.

I received a call just before lunch break telling me that Ruth had died. I rushed to Miss Delia's house. That's where they were living until the house became available. I got there in record- breaking time to find everyone waiting on Rip to show up. Miss Delia said she had heard them arguing earlier that morning. Rip stormed out of the house and speeded out of the driveway. Ruth had gotten up and prepared breakfast for her and Lib. The two worked at the same laundry and rode together. Lib would walk around from the projects she lived, they would eat together, have a drink together and leave for work. This morning she didn't wait for Lib to eat. She met her outside trying to explain that Rip had left. She began to convulse and felled. Lib got her inside the house. She complained about a headache. She started into the kitchen to prepare for work forgetting that she had already done that. Miss Delia convinced her to lie down. She called Gloria, her other daughter-in-law. When Gloria got there she had begun to convulse again. She was DOA at the Rowan Memorial Hospital.

I couldn't believe her death; she had so many plans for her and her girls. They were finally settling down after traveling for twenty years with Sergeant Rippy, her husband of twenty years, of the United States Army. Meme was borne in France thus came her nickname. Rip had asked for a divorce. She refused to agree with his terms. Her marriage to him had interrupted her college and her career. She had sacrificed for twenty years as a military wife and wasn't about to miss any of his retirement benefits. The following year Lib died and left five children the oldest about eighteen. These women were not only my sister-in-law's but my friends.

It was November 1961 when I met Joe's mother at his Brother William's house. We were, William, and his wife Gloria and me, sitting in his living room drinking "Old Crow", a whole fifth when I saw this tall slim elder woman coming towards the house. "Her comes mama," Joe said. "Oh, that's your mama, shouldn't we get this stuff off the table out of her sight," I asked, not wanting to be caught up in any drama. I knew it would be drama in my mama's house. "O don't worry about it, mama's coming to get her a little drink, Joe said as he got up to let her in. "Hey mama, come on in," he said, and meet my girlfriend; this is Shirley Sims from Spartanburg, SC. She's a student at Livingstone College. "What you doing over hear child and your folks sending you to college?" she asked disappointed in me for being there. She took her a drink, straight, took a swallow of water, and wiped across her mouth and took a seat next to me.

She began to tell me how she had to leave Georgia at the age of eighteen. She started by saying, "my daddy was from the Zulu tribe, and he was seven feet tall and couldn't go in the army because he was too tall. He and mama decided that every other one of us girls would go to school learn and teach the ones that didn't git to go. I was the other one and Maggie was the one to get educated. We were sharecroppers for old man Mote and he was the meanest old "white" man around. He came one evening and slapped mama because she hadn't picked her weight in cotton for that day. Mama tried to tell him how sick she was but he wouldn't listen. He continued to slap her when I jumped on his back and wrestled him off mama. He left swearing that he'd be back to deal with me and we knew what he meant. Papa and mama smuggled me out of Georgia and I hadn't been back since," she said with pride.

As she left I could see the sadness in her eyes, she had endured a lot of hardship in her lifetime but managed to walk with her head high. She was thirty-six before she had her first child. The doctors told her that she'd never bare a child because she only had one ovary. If she did it would never be a boy child. Being pregnant at thirty-six was a pleasant surprise. After Elisabeth was borne she met Bynum Tugman and fell in love with this tall handsome man and decided he had to be her husband, and she got what she wanted. Ruth was borne and then God blessed her with three sons, Joe Bynum, "Bud", George, "Babe Brother", William, and "Red" Tugman. God blessed her womb and gave her three seed carriers for the Tugman's. She was proud of her three sons as they grew up into men. Bud, she spoiled because he looked exactly like his daddy. She allowed him to get away with things that the girls didn't have a chance with. His sisters spoiled him also by catering to his every cry. She had great expectations for her sons, especially Joe being the oldest.

She was proud that he had finished high school and joined the United States Air Force. Bynum had died shortly after Babe Brother finished high school and went into the United States Navy and Red was a senior in high school. Red had quit school and taken over his daddy's job to help support the family. She insisted on Red finishing school. They job gave him a night shift and hired him permanent after graduation. He later retired from this plant after it passed through several ownerships and finally phased out his position after forty-six years with them.

She was proud to have me as a daughter – in – law and the mother of her three grandsons to carry the Tugman's seed. She was one of the wisest women I'd ever met. She had the high cheekbones, smooth latté complexion, and silky long hair like her Seminole grandmother, and a tall slim stature like her father. "Young Lady, everybody should have three things in life; a Bible, a piece of dirt, and a subscription of the Reader's Digest, she said with pride, I always study the word test and it helps me to understand what I'm reading when I read other books," while giving me the condensed book that she had just finished reading.

She worked hard to acquire her piece of dirt and pay for her old run down house. Bynum never took the time to fix up. He'd bootlegged to help keep things running for the family. He and his twin brother Cummie had moved from Lenoir, NC and settled in Salisbury looking for work with the railroad. Both ended up with other jobs that didn't pay as well. Theses twins had strong morals about supporting their family and did what was necessary to support them. Their brother, Fritz could make homebrew that frost like beer but he didn't have nothing on Miss Delia. She made perfume from rose petals of the rose bushes she grew, wine from the peels of the fruits from her garden and preserves, and corncob wine. She ran her house and Mrs. Corni house, which was the wife of one of the judges.

"Mama always said, " don't work for poor "white folks" cause they don't know no more than you do and they are jealous of what you got, plus they don't pay well." Mrs. Corni permitted her to bring her babies to work where she could watch them along with her children. She was very upset when our marriage failed. She came up during the period of time when men could whip there women and nothing would be done about it. They called it "putting them in their place"; Ben called it "cleaning off" when he would beat Helen.

Joe was taught how to handle problems by watching how daddy handled them. Daddy would be gone the entire weekend expecting her to run the house as well as the business. He wined and dined the women of the community. He and Cummie were good-looking men. Wherever they were there would be a flock of women looking for a favor or a drink or a date. The trouble for Bynum began when he returned home to face Delia. She was a feisty little lady and would stand up to Bynum physically anytime and most of the times hitting first. "You ain't gotta leave Bud, Bynum used to drag me down the street. He went with old Maggie Higgins, Addie's sister, for years but I told him that was one lie he told that I was going to make him be truthful," she was saying to me pleading.

"Miss Delia I just came for Steven, I've got the others in the car. I got them out of school and I'm going to Spartanburg and start a new life without Joe. If I stay here he'll soon kill me because the beatings are getting worst. Miss Delia he's even abusive to you, I've seen how he talks to you and I've seen him hit you. If he does that to you what'd you think he'll do to me?" I *was saying in defense of my leaving. "You always thought you were better than Bud, I knew that it wouldn't last," she said with sadness in her voice, I knew she didn't mean it but was hurt that I was leaving. She knew that I had to leave and could leave because I had my education. The lack of education was what trapped her into a loveless marriage with five children, as it did with Helen.*

"Be ye not unequally yoked goes so much further than having the same beliefs; its education, hobbies, goals, money, and so much more. Because neither husband was educated beyond high school my education was a threat to their manhood. It was a struggle to maintain your intellect when you are in the company of non- educated people. My social friends were older women who had daughters my age and who never graduated from high school and I was always in a mode of proving "I didn't think that I was better than they" attitude.

Man is no more than who he thinks he is.
Man is no more than what he thinks he is.
Only God knows the true thoughts of man.
Only God knows the true heart of man.
O' glory, O' glory, O 'glory.

The mouth speaks while the heart bleeds and pleads.
O' I'm fine, and all is well, instead of hear my cry.
How are you, instead of who are you?
O' glory, O' glory, O' glory.
O' glory, O' glory, O' glory.

Where are your honor and majesty countenance?
Where are your strength and your power?
Where are your grace and mercy?
Did mercy rob justice?
O' glory, O' glory, O 'glory.

Glorify Me the Father as you will the Son.
For the son of man is no greater than the Son of God.
Glorify the Son and you glorify the Father.
Glorify the Father and you glorify the Son.
O' glory, O' glory, O' glory.

Is the wisdom of man greater than the power of God?
Is the knowledge of man deeper than God's?
Wisdom comes from God and so does knowledge,
Understanding is the wisdom of the knowledge of God.
O' glory, O' glory, O' glory.

Glory and Honor and majesty are his countenance.
Strength and power is his will for man.

Grace sufficed mercy and robbed death of its sting and death of the grave.
The spoken word became the living word, Jesus Christ.
O' glory, O' glory, O' glory.   Shirley Sims Gray© July 24, 2005

After giving up my teaching position and settling in Salisbury, my life became routine and in a slump. I wasn't satisfied being a housewife; raising my kids and others too. I'd done this all of my life and wanted more than this. Joe seemed to be satisfied and all of his associates with working for the upholstery plant, being paid on Friday and spending the weekend gambling. This lifestyle was ok for a single man. These men had gotten caught up in taking care of only themselves, living off woman including their mothers. Joe wasn't a good poker player but a compulsive gambler and gambled on anything and everything. His future was going to be great "if and when" he makes that big hit, he knew it would come; he did what he chose with his paycheck, after all he had worked for it.

He sent money home when he was in the military and sent for it sometimes before it reached home. It came through an allotment from his military pay. Mrs. Delia tried saving it for him to have something when he got out but his gambling habit wouldn't allow it. Mommas are always the last to know or admit what their children are doing especially their oldest who should be setting an example for the others. He never took responsibility for his family that is his three sons, his daughter and I. Having him as a husband was like having another child to feed, clothe, and give shelter to. He didn't pay rent or anybody else and could find your money no matter where you hid it. When he did give me money I had to spend it quickly because he came back for it. Many times I've awaked to find the money and him gone; back to the gambling table. "You should have used it when I gave it to you, I thought you didn't need it since it was still on the dresser." Would be his comment when I confronted him.

We moved from Standish Street where all of the Livingstone College students came who knew me, to Hawkins town. I had hopes that our marriage would get better. I was supervisor of Cytology and he was working for Hoechst Fiber, a new plant with benefits and salaries that topped all other plants. It was a rent to own and our first home. The two salaries were sufficient for the new life style, except Joe continued to use his to satisfy his needs and habits. I made several attempts to set up a plan where he would contribute to the financial needs to run this house, only to be outsmarted by him. He was supposed to put one hundred dollars a week in the checking account. He told me that he did and even asked for a deposit slip each week for three weeks. Checks began to bounce from the grocery store to the mortgage payment. This was the straw that broke the Camel's back. It was all I could take, it had been eleven years of this kind of living and I was a bit feed up with it.

I began to make arrangements to leave after realizing I would never get him out of the house. I'd begin counseling sessions at the local mental health clinic after calling the dial HELP number. When I learned why my checks were bouncing and Joe attitude about it, my reaction to this frightened me. I was calm and had a feeling that I could not recognized, it's as if the feeling took control. I called and asked how I could get my husband out of my house and out of the lives of my children. I began to tell them of his gambling problem and the effects it was having on the children and I. I couldn't understand why I had to suffer and give up everything I had worked for just to rid myself of this burden, my husband Joe.

How many times have I started over in my life was a question that came into my mind. I began to go through my mind to count. I realized that each day is a time to start over. Each year was an opportunity to continue with where you started the year before, or start something new. Each day should be a time of adventure into the goodness of God and all of his glory. I awake about four o'clock am, sometimes I try to lay a little longer but the body demands to be up. The mind has already booted up. Four o'clock in the morning when you can hear only the sounds of nature, the tinkling of the bell, the hoot of the owl, the squeak of the frog, the crowing of the rooster, the creeping of the bugs and the radar signals giving the birds their command for the day.

Material things became an important factor in my career as it was used as a measuring stick for success. How big is the house, what model of the car, where did you purchase your furniture, whose name is on your clothes, how educated are you, are all measurements for success. Naked I came and naked I'll leave yet we hold on to things as if we can take it with us. We fought all of our lives for our rights to do what? We died for our rights to do what? Was it to pursue the right to liberty and justice for all?

When we start over generally we are speaking of replacing material things with more material things. Not wanting to give up what I had worked for was more important to me than making this abusive marriage work. My mind had to figure out how to kill two birds with one stone, keep my possessions and get rid of him. I had just purchased my first home, had a professional job, two cars, and active in the "church", member of the Livingstone Alumni Chapter, and yet my life was miserable. It was what was going on in the inside of the home. When I moved to the new home my intentions were to leave Joe. Not only did I need to escape from him but also his daughter, Laney.

She had tried telling me about "something" rubbing on her leg while she slept. I thought it was another one of her complaints about having to share Scooter's bed. She gave her bed to Claudia and took over his bed. I was awaken that night by her screaming, "Git outta here." Joe came crawling up the hallway and felled into the bed. I tried to wake him by shaking and calling his name but he wouldn't respond. I went into the room where the children slept and found Laney crying. "What happened Laney?" I asked. "Daddy had his hand under the covers rubbing my legs," she said. I had to leave the room because I became nauseated. I went back to the room and tried to rouse Joe and he would not respond. "Go back to sleep Laney, we'll talk about this in the morning," I said to her as I went to the living room and remained there the rest of the night in a state of confusion. I should have called the police, this is hindsight. I never called the police even when he beat me and I never knew why.

The next morning Joe got up as if nothing happened. "Why were you in the children's room last night and why were you bothering Laney?" I asked him boldly while the children slept. "Woman you always have been a crazy motherfucker, your own mama and daddy said you didn't have good sense. I'll put you and Laney's ass in the crazy house if I hear any of this shit anymore," he said with a threat that caused chills to come over my body. We never talked about it anymore, I did not know how to defend Laney because I couldn't defend myself, I knew I could not tell but I didn't know why I could not tell. I was sick to the pit of my stomach and began planning and preparing to leave and save my children from this monster.

If he'd molest his own daughter, slap his mother, and take commodity food from his sister Lib who had five children and a single parent, what were my chances of surviving? I knew I had to do something to keep him away from Laney; I would do things to entice him and make sure that his sexual appetite was satisfied by during whatever he wanted; he was a freak, a sadist, a rapist, and everything except a lover. He didn't know how to love me or make love to me.

I see why Helen wasn't able to protect me because she couldn't protect herself either. Ben had taken her as a fourteen-year-old child and impregnated her. Made her a mother at fifteen. He not only stole her virginity but he stole her childhood, her teen age years, her young adult years.
When he died she was a sixty-four year old woman. She been a slave to this man for over forty years and ten children. All he left her for that was a big red ass old Cadillac. She had endured hardship and embarrassment from Ben. He woke her up one night when he brought some of the boys' home for a break of all night drinking, "Helen git up and come in here," he said demanding her. She rushed and got up looking for a dress to cover her nightgown thinking Bennie must want me to fix him something to eat. She came in surprised that he had others with him. "What do you want me to fix Bennie, there's souse meat in the refrigerator," she was saying when he interrupted. "Na'll, I don't want nothing to eat. Look at her boys, that's da way you keep em, big and barefooted," he said leading the laughter and all others joining in. This embarrassed her. Her disgust for him grew even deeper. I never saw a gesture of affection shown between the two not even a word of affection.

My mother's life was made a living hell by my daddy who took advantage of a fourteen-year -old girl that was at the prime of puberty. Her family moved from the Glen Springs area of Spartanburg County where they had lived as sharecropper. They were moving on up. Coming to Spartanburg where there was work other than in the cotton fields. Her daddy, Roland Jones, had gotten a job at the fertilized mill and they got to live in the company's house. Their house was the biggest on the line with a commercial toilet seat and running water across the street. Pa moved the family that consisted of Notie Jones, Ma, Benjamin or "Beechie", Southern, Lucille, Marion and Helen, my mama. Della, the oldest and Laura were married and not living with them when they moved.

Next-door was the Sims, Mr. Irvin and Miss Mary, a sophisticated family who owned all of the land except where the fertilize mill sat, although they may have owned it at one time. They owned their house and several more. The community was named after them, The Sims Chapel Community, The Sims Chapel Methodist Church, The Sims Chapel School, and the Sims Chapel Road. My daddy, Bennie Ervin Sims, was there first grandchild, and his daddy Albert was Irvin's first child, first son of six sons and four daughters.

My mother and her sister Marion were still in school when they moved. Helen said when they changed school they would put them back in the grade they had just finished. Sims Chapel School only went to the six grades and to go further you'd have to go to city school or down to Roebuck, if you wanted to go further. She and Marion went to the six grades as the new girls in town and the prettiest girls in the whole community. They looked like twins and even dressed alike. They were each other's best friend and shared every secret with each other. They were more matured than the other six-graders, because they were older and the older boys and men were attracted to them.

Marion and my mother were seduced and impregnated by men ten years or more their senior shortly after the move. My mama was fourteen and Marion was sixteen. Della Mae, Marion's daughter was born July 2nd 1941 and I September 18th 1941. 1941 was not a good year to have babies out of wedlock. You were ostracized and labeled as someone you don't bother with because they'd had a baby. February 1942, seven months after Della Mae was borne Marion died from pneumonia they say, but I bet it was from a broken heart and broken dreams. My mother lost her best friend, her sister, her rock and she was lost, confused, frighten, sixteen with no visible means of taking care of a child. She was the youngest of her siblings and had no experience of attending to a baby. She had helped out a bit with Bennie Mae, her oldest sister Della's daughter but she was only six years older than her.

Taking care of a seven-month-old baby is a full time task for my grandmother who is also raising her nine-year-old granddaughter, Bennie Mae. Her mother, Della had left her with my grandmother when she was still a baby and left her son Roosevelt, a toddler with the Glenn's, her husband's family. It didn't seem fair to my grandmother who had raised her two sons and five girls and now she's raising her grandbabies. Raising Della Mae kept her daughter Marion's memories fresh in her mind. She too was looking forward to living in this big old company's house with Roland making more money than he'd ever made. There were jobs for her two sons also. World war 11 had broken out in Germany and her sons were drafted into the war, her daughter died at age eighteen, and left a seven-month-old baby and her youngest daughter, fifteen is a mother.

Helen had been spoiled by all of her older brothers and sisters. She was daddy's little girl and used to being the center of attention. She was used to receiving attention from older boys who were friends with her older brother. The younger boys didn't interest her. She met Ben through her brother Beechie who was dating his sister Fannie Mae. Ben took advantage of the friendship to get next to Helen. "I bet Ben raped Helen because she was only fourteen when she got pregnant with me," I was saying to Bennie Mae, my cousin who was six years younger than Helen and eight years younger than Marion. "No child, I was peeping through the pine knot hole in the door and say them. Horace and Bennie were on top of Helen and Marion on the same bed in the same room. That's when they came up pregnant," Bennie Mae said.

I changed her destiny in life. She too, as all women do, had dreamed of marrying her prince charming and living happily ever after but Ben didn't want any part of that dream. He already had a little girl, Jessie by Nan English and didn't marry her. He was having too much fun to be tied down married.

It couldn't have been easy for her at home with Ma and all of the stress she was under. She made Helen take care of me because she had to take care of Della Mae. Ma was a strict disciplinary with her girls and firmly believed if you make your bed hard you have to sleep in it. Ben, been the player he was, found his way back into Helen's life again and again impregnating her and Miss Nancy Artison. They lived directly across the street from where he lived. He was the rooster among the women folks and had no regard or no care where he left his seeds. "One baby we can handle but two you've got to go was the attitude of the times, two babies make you married". The other women only had one baby and were older women in their early twenties like Ben, and were more ready for marriage than she was. She had managed very well with me and was actually making plans for her and me, maybe one of those sleep-in jobs up North like a lot of Black women were doing at that time.

It was mostly the rich Jews in New York that would hire the "colored girls' as sleep-in maids. It worked well for many, getting them out of the sharecropper's fields. They had free room and board, two days a week off, and most of all they were in New York City, the land of "milk and honey" for the "colored folks." It gave them the opportunity to save money and help back home. Ben's mother, Miss Geneva, had several sisters in New York as sleep-in maids and brothers in Pittsburg with the steel mills. She and Aunt Emma had to stay home to take care of their mother. She changed that destiny when she met and married Albert Sims, the oldest son of Mr. Ervin Sims. He owned every inch of land in the Sims Chapel Community. This marriage put her in a different class from her siblings and certainly above all of the common "colored folk" that lived around her.

Bennie Ervin Sims, born October 28th 1916, the first born of Albert and Geneva Sims. The first borne grandchild of Ervin and Mary Sims, owners of the Sims Chapel Community. "Bennie was a spoiled child, honey, it wasn't nothing he wanted Papa wouldn't give him," Aunt Della would tell me. She and Ben were the same age. He stole all of the attention from her and all the rest of them. Papa's hope was in Bennie that he would continue his legacy. His six sons weren't interested and his girls had married men that wasn't interested either. He tried mentoring Bennie. His greatest fault with Bennie was catering to his every want. He crippled him by growing him up fast without any sense of responsibility," Aunt Della rehearsed to me many times when I would question her about my heritage.

Ben and Helen's marriage was a shotgun wedding. It's when the daddy and brothers of the girl grabs the responsible boy or man that got her pregnant and force them to marry while the girl's family holds onto the shotgun. At fourteen she lost her virginity to this man. Two years later she lost her freedom to live her life. She lost absolute control of her life, pregnant, married, and on her way to Boise, Idaho with a husband who was forced to marry her. The move was the best thing that ever happened to her and for her. Her hope returned only to be lost when Ben insisted on moving back home to mama after his stay in the military. They returned to Spartanburg to his mama's house.

He continued to live the same lifestyle he'd lived before he was drafted into the military; fast cars, women, gambling, drinking, hustling. If he had missed the draft he would have never left Spartanburg or his mama's house, there he had no responsibilities. He said he could be gone for an entire weekend and his mother would save his portion of the food from each meal that was made while he was out. Ben had a domineering mother who ran things including his daddy. He watched his daddy out of frustration drink himself to death. He never live up to neither his fathers' standards nor his wife's. She was a greedy woman always nagging him about getting his share of the inheritance. A woman never satisfied.

My great-granddaddy had given them the house and two acres of land to raise their family but she wanted more. This had been the original family home. He built it for his family. It was used for a school after building a larger house on the hill on Sims Chapel Road. The house was the school he started for his children and any others that could come after leaving the fields. He gave land to the community. He dedicated the land to God for a church and a school. He building the school beside the church when they were married sometimes in 1916 just before my daddy was borne.

The Sims' were not only wealthy but they were light skinned also, giving them an edge over her family who were truly Black. Bennie, her first-born was a little brown skinned baby but resembled his daddy, and so were his sister Mary, who died young, and Eddie. Sam, the youngest son, and Fannie Mae the youngest daughter were a little lighter. Uncle Ed was the middle son and the darkest. She really didn't like. He'd get drunk and tell her that he knew she didn't like him. She detested him because he drank just like his daddy. She didn't include him in her will.

From the very beginning she began claiming what was rightfully her husband's and children. She interfered in all of their lives by dictating whom they could or couldn't associate with. She didn't like the Jones' next door or the Artison' across the street and definite not the English's Bennie ran around with. Mr. Artison looked like a white man. He had a son Willie and a daughter Louise that looked like him and a "black" daughter Nancy and a "black" son, James that looked like his wife who had died from measles. Ben liked the "black" Nancy. All of the English's were cold "black" and the Jones' were a little better, but they didn't have "nothing".

Bennie had a car even as a teenager his granddaddy bought him. This made him very popular with the girls as well as the boys. Bennie had babies in all of these households and they all were "Black" except me. She despised me just like she did the Jones because" they didn't come from nothing." Even her daughter Fannie Mae gave birth to a black child and his daddy was light-skinned and had good hair. None of the fifteen grandchildren are as light-skinned as I am; yet she never liked me because I was the "outside" child. She never accepted the fact that Bennie married Helen and me.

When Ben moved us into his mama's house, my life took a turn for the worst. I was the outside child as far as she was concerned and whatever Bennie had, "won't go to them Jones' because of this little bastard child." I'm in a house where nobody loves me. I lost my place in the family, the "first" to the "outside."

Whoa! Who stole my place?
Whoa! Who stole my birthright?
I got the seed of the Sims
I'm the purebred of the line.

No one took up for me but blamed me for everything. My mother's constant, "Sit down Shirley," still ring in my ears sometimes. It was always about not disturbing anyone or getting in any ones way. I was a five year old surrounded by people who didn't hesitate to let me know how much they disliked me. I would slip off next to the other grand mama's, Notie, Helen's mother, but she didn't have time for me. She was raising my five years old cousins Della Mae, and a teen-aged granddaughter, Bennie Mae. I can remember feeling alone and scared, and always in somebody's way, "with your o "red" self." I always had something someone else wanted, "With your o "red" self;" Whatever it was it always ended with, "your o "red" self." There was always some man around touching and putting their hands on me at my grandma's house and Miss Geneva's house.

I was never anyone's little girl.
I was never anyone's favorite,
I was never anyone's pet, but I was a peeve. Shirley Jean Jones © 2005

Miss Geneva had her back porch screened in and made a community store out of it. She sold drinks to the workers at the fertilize mill and other snacks. On Friday she sold hot dogs. All the families on the street bought from her and some had credit with her. Della Mae and Bennie Mae would come and get them a drink on Ma's bill. Jackie Boy could get one just for the asking. He was told that he didn't have to share with me. No one ever bought one for Shirley, the little bastard, Fannie Mae would call me.

One day I lied and told Miss Geneva that the other grandmamma said I could get a drink on her bill. She gave it to me but asked my grandma about it. Off course I'd lied. The drink wasn't worth the punishment. Helen sent me there once to get some drinks. I was so excited to do this. I skipped back swinging the bottles behind me when they met and broke. I was terrified when I saw blood and began to run opposite from home. I knew the beating was going to be worse than the cut. I needed to get away from the harshness of Helen. She caught me and slapped my butt a couple of times before she saw the blood. Thank God she saw it, it stopped the slapping. I don't remember having a drink of my own until years later.

Everybody on our street was "black" as cold, except the Scotts and the Artison that was related in some manor, I don't remember how. I do remember Mrs. Scotts' funeral being held in the home and all of the Artison relatives came home for the funeral. The funeral was held in their home not a church like everyone else did and it wasn't on a Sunday either. I don't know what Mrs. Scott's religion was but Mr. Scott was Superintendent of our Sunday school. We used to have Sunday school in his home when the Community Baptist Church was first organized in 1952 by Mr. J. W. Walkers. Mr. Will Atchison put all of the Baptist out of the church.

All of their children were either older than me or too young for me to play with. My only playmates were Jackie Boy, Della Mae, Bobby Jean, my cousins, and Hazel and Nanny Hunter, all dark skinned and hated my light skinned complexion and me. When I became a teenager I would sit in the sun beginning March trying to darken my legs for the summer to wear shorts so they wouldn't make fun of "dem old white legs." Children are the cruelest because they speak *what they hear the grown-ups say behind the door. They without remorse justify whatever they do or say to you with the same attitude the grown-ups have against you.*

My Aunt Della always told me that I would be the one to "Carry Papa's legacy. I was more Sims than any of Bennie's children, not only did I have the complexion but I had their brains. Papa taught us all to read and play the piano, she would tell me, we would gather after dinner and Papa would school us; Papa was respected both by Black and White." During my career I had an eighty-seven year old "white" client who knew my great granddaddy Ervin and my granddaddy Albert Sims.

"Yes I knew Mr. Sims, he was a fine gentleman, and he's the only person for miles who had a car. Yes, I knew them both and you are their daughter, bless you my child because Mr. Sims left you a treasure," old Mrs. Smith said after I told her I remembered her when I was a small child. She was a small child when my granddaddy died but remembers the relationship he and her daddy had.

I had returned to Spartanburg, SC with my three sons and my stepdaughter with only the clothes on our backs and $100.00 in my pocket. I had to leave earlier than planned. When Joe realized I was leaving he went into a rage nightly with threats and accusations. I began to fear for my life. I knew I could not wait any longer. If I didn't leave now I'd never be able to leave. I had prepared for the move by getting a job with The Spartanburg Memorial Hospital as a Cytotechnologist, being the first "black" to be hired in their laboratory. I had a realtor looking for a house to move into. I did not want to move in my mothers' house. I had retained an attorney for my divorce and child custody.

I had earned over a thousand dollars in pay, vacation pay and a little savings and had closed out all debt in my name. It was in November just a few days before Thanksgiving. Ben wasn't a happy camper having my boys and me in his house even for a short period of time. I worked eight hours a day at the hospital and five to six hours an evening at H&R Block doing income taxes. I had had all but the last week of training by H&R Block in Salisbury and the information was still fresh. I had no problem being hired. By December I had purchased a car and made a deal to purchase a home for my boys and I. Joe was surprised at how well I was doing on my own. He would not believe that I was doing it on my own. The pressure from Joe and the pressure from Ben to get out of his house and his constant reminder that he wasn't going to "feed my kids or me" put me in an uncomfortable position. I had to protect my children not only from Joe but from Ben also. He hated my children just as he did me and just like me, they never did anything to him.

Moving back to Spartanburg was a mistake I've regretted many times, it was a step backward. After I began raising my sons and realized the importance of loving them and teaching them, they became my reason for continuing on. It was my plans never to have any children but God saw different and I'm glad he did. I can't imagine my life without them. Joe knew how important the boys were to me and used that to control me. When I would mention leaving, and I learned early not to mention, he would threaten to kill them and me. This among other factors kept me there. The other factors can be summed up in one word, FEAR. I gave in to the power of fear. They say, "no one has any more power over you than you give them." I don't know who "they" are but I do know that your will power can be taken away and you never be aware that you have given it away, some call it "brainwashing".

Joe's physical abuse began December 7, 1962. I had managed to earn a few dollars sewing for my sister-in-law Gloria and using her sewing machine. I had her to take me shopping for fabrics to make curtains for the living room. I found a bargain and bought enough fabric to make draperies that draped from the corner of one window to the corner of the other window, it was gorgeous I thought. Joe came home after having been gone since the night before gambling, tired, hungry, and broke. "What's all of this shit in the floor Shirley, I ain't going be living in no messy house, so git your ass in here and clean it up now," he growled without a greeting or explanation, heading to the kitchen. My sisters-in-laws had been washing all day using the wringer washer I had in the kitchen. The washer was still pulled out and he couldn't get into the kitchen. "Joe how do you like the draperies?" I asked as he came back to the living room. For an answer I was slapped across the face. Until this day I cannot describe the pain that my spirit experienced. It became a broken spirit December 7th 1962.

Victims of molestation and physical abuse becomes subjective to the emotions the acts bring with them. They control your destiny by developing protective measures against the pain it brings. The protected measure manifests itself in different manners that's determined by the circumstances and which pain needs protecting. These manifestations are controlled by the subconscious mind that has shield the pain from the conscious mind and the conscious becomes unconsciously. Joe's physical abuse aroused a pain that was buried deep in the subconscious mind and submission was my best protector.

You do things to please but nothing pleases.
You blame yourself and nobody else.
You wonder what mood is safe and which is not.
Then the lights goes out and none are safe.

The physical abuse continued and escalated. Each time I became more submissive until I lost all of my will power and became subjective to the controller. It took eleven years to get strength enough to leave and even more strength not to return and even harder without the most precious things in my life, my children.

Joe used them as a pawn to control me. He'd take them while I worked. If I wanted to see them again I'd better come back to Salisbury. It was the hardest thing I've ever done in my life. It didn't matter leaving all of the material things behind such as the house and all of its furniture or even the job, these are replaceable, but not the children. Joe had become abusive to them also and had continued his peeking on his daughter Laney who moved out and lived with "uncle Red. I prayed that God would watch over my boys, if they had been girls I'd never left them. I never wanted my boys to grow up in a home without a good male image of a father or a husband. I prayed that all of the things they witnessed would be used as a guide rule of what not to do to your family.

My family in Spartanburg had no idea how badly I was hurting and how alone and lost I felt. I felt like a failure; a broken marriage with children is like a death without a burial or without closure. I became a bitter person and internalized my emotions. I tried pretending I didn't have any children. I didn't talk about them and tried not to think about them. That was an impossibility.

I ventured into a lifestyle that was foreign to me trying to find where I belonged. I'd been a mother since I was seven years old and all I knew to do is take care of others before you take care of yourself. I began to accommodate men whom I knew wanted me but never dared to say anything to me. I never took anything from them and never asked them for anything as a matter of fact I gave to them. None of them can claim they bought me or took me, and none of them can claim a love for them or from me, because I was without feeling. I used this body that had been molested, abused, bruised, used, mutilated, manipulated, and controlled them. I was like the black widow of sex. Man has used sex as a controlling factor in my life all of my life so consciously I disassociated me from sex; it's not who I am or even what I am.

Marriage was a protective measure from the pain of being raped again. Joe never thought that he had raped me, it was consensual sex, he said. It was more manipulative sex than consensual sex. A twenty-seven year old sex veteran over a nineteen-year-old college student looking for love and attention from a man. Joe's attention helped me to hide the pain I was suffering from the abortion to come to college, and the separation and lies I'd told the father of the baby. College didn't have the same meaning after the abortion as it did before the pregnancy. It was going to be the means of escape from the loveless environment I'd grown up in. The escape became secondary to the birth of my child but not for Helen. I'd always regretted not speaking up for myself. I was sixteen-years old and submissive to her.

I never argued or talked back with her as Mary Alice did. I refused to be disrespectful to her. I would find a quiet place and privately cry. The grief for the loss of my little girl was internalized. It was never mentioned, as if it never happened. I took this grief and this lie into my marriage. I blamed the abortion for the miscarriage of my twin boys. The conscious mind told me that I was not worthy to be loved by God or anybody else because of the abortion. I had asked God to punish me. Every time something bad happened to me I received it as a punishment from God.

I had no problem being loyal to my husbands because marriage was a safe haven for me. It protected me from other men who wanted sex from me. Once I told Joe about one of our "friend's, Charles Weldon, bringing me a message from another man. I told him thinking he'd protect me from this man. Instead he got upset with me and blamed me; that was the last time I told him anything; I didn't tell him about the wrestling match with my brother-in law Rippy, or James Crowder, his sister Lib's boyfriend or any others and there were others.

Sex is sex regardless of who it's with, if there is no love, and mine was without love both times, it's just something that's expected of you when you are married. It was something that I consented to most of the times because it would only last for a few minutes if I didn't resist. The times I did resist I was raped. Like not giving in when my baby was only two weeks old or when he was drunk and will "be there" so long it would irritate me. It would be difficult to walk for a few days. I stayed raw from the continued recurrence of yeast infection/ bladder infection/trichomonas, and even crabs shortly after the marriage.

Joe worked at the VA Hospital in Salisbury, NC, in dietary department. To work at the VA was something to the people there because of the "benefits." It was a government hospital. The one in Salisbury was for soldiers with mental problems stemming from the wars or Post Traumatic Syndrome Behavior/ shell shock. I picked him up from his day shift job. He asked me to stop at a drug store. When we got home he began complaining about "those nasty white folks" and how you can catch anything behind them. He took from the bag a tube of ointment. He asked me to rub my private parts good with it and he was going to do the same. When I asked him why we were doing this, he raised his hand as if to strike me and I stepped back puzzled. "Just do what I ask you to do Shirley and stop asking so many damn questions," he said reaching me the tube. The next morning he ran a tub of water and when he sat in it many little dead bugs were in his bathe water and then ordered me to do the same. I had about four little dead bugs to fall from me. "I guess I didn't catch them from you," he said with disappointment in his voice. Why would he think that he had gotten them from me? He was my husband and the only man I'd been with since the first time he slept with me. This situation was never spoken off anymore.

My situation was worst here than it was at home with Ben and Helen and all their chillums. I was embarrassed to be a college graduate living with the threat of eviction, the cutting off of our utilities, sometimes in the same day, the bill collector coming every day, the empty refrigerator, and a husband that beats me. I received this as God's punishment for the abortion and the lie I took into the marriage and even the marriage itself was a punishment. Joe hated being married. He only married me after the insistence from his mama and sisters. They blamed him for "messing up" my life and to rectify it insisted on him marrying me. September 28th 1962, seven weeks after he married me I miscarried identical twin boys. He despised me for losing the one thing that would have made him proud. His daddy too if he had been living. His daddy was an identical twin. I became consumed with grief and guilt of my own for losing my babies.

Some has said that the miscarriage was my "out" of the marriage and I should have left Joe then. I could not see me walking out of my marriage no matter how bad it was. I felt that I owed Joe something for miscarrying his sons. I wasn't given the opportunity to name my babies nor see them, and again I internalized my grief and continued on with a determination that life was not going to steal my dream. My plans to be a doctor was interrupted and I became a biology and science schoolteacher. The teaching career lasted about three years and again fate changed my plans. Finding myself once again in a losing environment; Joe's gambling addiction and drinking, friends old enough for my mother, and surrounded by people who were satisfied with where they were in life and putting me down for wanting more.

Single women with babies on welfare were a common and accepted way for many but not for me. When I returned to Spartanburg after leaving Joe I was given the run down on how to get welfare and get food stamps. When I refused the family said I thought I was too good to get on welfare. Why would I do that with the profession I had? They had zero understanding of the profession and just considered it as something to waste my education. They knew nothing of the sacrifice it took to have this profession and this career. Nor did they know of the honors I had received as a Cytotechnologist, or the sacrifice I made to become a certified tax preparer. When I stopped teaching school is when I began to "waste my education."

When I realized that this professional pay was not sufficient to support our lifestyle I took on a second job at H&R Block to supplement my income. I did some taxes on my own. When I realized the money I could make on my own I stopped working for Block and set up my own business. I put up one sign in Adolphus Brown's Barber Shop and had so much business it paid me to miss a few days of work from the hospital. At the end of the tax season I had earned enough money to buy a car and put a down payment on a home for my boys and me. Buying the house had been delayed because I used the monies I had when I first returned home to bail Sandra out of jail and to pay for her an attorney.

She had called me at my job and asked to use my car. She needed to take care of some business at Spartanburg Methodist College. She had taken some courses there and needed to clear up a bill. Sandra knew the importance I put on education and knew that that lie would work with me so I gladly loaned her my car. She was there to pick me up from work on time and bragged about the full tank of gas she had put into the car. I dropped her off at her home and checked in for work at H&R Block on Church Street. They sent me to the office on Forrest Street. I called to let Helen know of the change of location. My boys were at her house. I had begun working with my first client when the phone rang for me. "Shirley, there's two detectives here looking for you, they say your car was involved in a shooting and a robbery and they want to come over and ask you a few questions," Helen was saying nervously. "No, tell them I'll come to them," I said hanging up the phone. "Sir, I'm sorry but I've got an emergency, I'll get one of the other consultants to take care of you," I was saying as I went to tell the manager I was leaving and why. I didn't wait for an answer as I rushed from the office trying to hold my composure. I left the job and stopped at Sandra's house that was in route to Helen's house.

I couldn't imagine Sandra being involved in a shooting and robbery and was ready for any explanation from her. Sandra was my pride, I'd taught her to say mama and daddy. She was the smartest little girl. She would try to teach Albert and Angela Spanish she was learning in school. She was only six or seven years old when Joe and I married. She would sit on Joe's lap as soon as we showed up. She was such a lovable little girl, how can this be? "Sandra, get your coat on, we've got to go out to Helen's, there are two detectives there saying my car was involved in a shooting and robbery," I was saying crying. "O that nigger must have done that when I let him use the car to get some beer," she said with a straight face. I had knocked at least five minutes before she answered the door. I had seen movement when I drove up so I knew someone was there. "Get your coat so you can go and get this thing straighten out," I said with relief. I waited downstairs for another ten or fifteen minutes. "Sandra, hurry so we can get this over, I need to get back to work," I called out. She came down the stairs dressed differently. I was so nervous I could hardly drive, my legs were shaking so badly. As we entered the house it was unusually quiet. "Hello, I am Shirley Tugman and this is my sister Sandra Smith, I said with pride knowing that this thing was about to go away. "Hello Miss Tugman, I'm Norwood Flower and this is Mr. McGowan, and Sandra Smith you are under arrest," he was saying as he handcuffed her. "No don't do that, listen to her story," I pleaded. "Ok Sandra tell us what happened and where is Ken," Norwood said.

She told them the same story she'd told me about the boy borrowing the car to get some beer and must have done it then. "Sandra we are going to take you downtown for further questioning," as he escorted her out of the house and placed her in the patrol car. "Don't worry Sandra, I'm going to follow so you'll have a ride home," I was telling her as I got in my car.

I was disappointed that no one else came with me. Ben had yelled, "Take her on to jail," after she told her story. I was the only one that believed her. I had not only missed her teen years but all of the others also. I was not around to meet their boyfriends or their friends, or observe their progress in school, or to teach anyone anymore. I was too busy trying to survive my marriage. Sandra had become pregnant at fifteen and married Kenneth Smith the father and by seventeen they had two children, Michelle and Kenneth, Jr., "Pete". Ken's mama, Willie Mae, was a hustling woman and had raised Ken in this environment. He drove a blue Mustang, had money in his pocket, and was shooting heroin. Ken had only been out of prison a few months when this situation happened. While he was there serving time Willie Mae was sneaking drugs in to him and she was selling to the inmates. They set her up with an undercover for a sell and she fell for the trap. It cost her eighteen months in prison. Sandra was pregnant with "Pete" when they arrested Willie Mae. Helen had to go to Columbia to pick Sandra up, they confiscated the car also. "Pete" was born that night. I paid Sandra's bail to get her out of jail the next day. I couldn't imagine her being in jail. I could only concentrate on what to do to help her.

The nonchalant attitude from the family was just as shocking as Sandra's life of crime. Everyone seemed to be involved in something illegal with "Poochie" being the kingpin. All of the girls were involved in some sort of drug, marijuana or cocaine, using and selling, and gambling, as was my two younger brothers and my nephew Ronnie. Rick and Ronnie were only thirteen when I returned home, still in junior high school. Angela was high school and Albert had dropped out of school. I began to feel that I had failed them. If I had been able to follow my dream and my plans they would not have been in this situation. Helen couldn't help them because she never experienced the peer pressure that teens go through. As a young mother she had skipped over the teen years responsibilities to adulthood responsibilities.

There is a process of growing up, baby, toddler, child, teen, and adult. Each step is a preparation for the next step. The lumps and bumps of life are the growing pains that one must experience to reach maturity and be productive citizens. Helen went from child to adulthood because a selfish spoiled man, Bennie Ervin Sims, robbed her of her teen year experiences. She never experienced high school with the prom and other teen aged girl's giggles, shared secrets, dating or the thrill of doing something foolish and getting away with it. She never experienced walking through the fairgrounds on "colored day" with a date, or going to the movies or strolling to church with friends and singing on the youth choir. The transformation from child to adulthood is as the mother hen helping the chick peck its way out of its shell, it handicaps.

It seemed that the teaching stopped when I left home. I had taught Helen many things such as baking a cake. Miss Viola taught me yet she would allow the younger ones to make fun that I couldn't cook. I taught her how to lay a pattern on the fabric because I could read and understand the directions and knew what the symbols meant. She figured out the sewing directions by looking at something similar whereas I could read and follow the directions for sewing it, yet I would seek her approval to only get a nod. I tried telling her how not to get pregnant after I returned from college majoring in biology and learned the process of reproduction.

When I returned to Spartanburg no one could help me because they all needed help. "Poochie" was King Pin, Pat was teaching at USCS as a nurse instructor, smoking pot, gambling, and shacking with a punk named Bill. Lane was teaching PE at one of the elementary schools, smoking and snorting cocaine, divorced, single parent, and gambling. Jackie was working after finishing some data processing course, single parent, smoking pot, gambling. Sandra was married and now on her way to prison, Albert, Angela, Rick and Ronnie were still at home and they all were doing drugs. When I told Helen, who was now working out of the home herself, that her baby Rick was doing drugs and selling them at school, he made me be a liar and she believed him. It was the first time Angela "told me off". "Just cause you da oldest don't mean you can come 'hear and tell us what to do with your old fashion self, she said, and anyway you ain't got no sense and you ain't never had any." She was fifteen and I was thirty-three. "Poochie had told me, in her presence that she had more sense than I did and knew better than I how to take care of herself plus she had heard it all of her life how crazy I was.

I had to get back to the business of gaining custody of my boys and finding a place for us to live. We were in Ben and Helen's house. Ben wasn't a happy camper with us there. I had used most of my money helping Helen to pay Sandra's bail and her an attorney. She, Helen and I showed up for her court date. Everyone else went there merry way including Ben, who would go to the court house daily, to see what was what, but didn't come to help Sandra. Others that didn't come justified it by saying what she shouldn't have done. To my amazement I had sisters and brothers that were all for self, and you if it doesn't take anything from them. I could not believe that they did not support each other but competed against each other, four teenaged girls at one time, Pat, Lane, Jackie, and Sandra.

I had left Salisbury with only the clothes on my back as well as the children. My three bedrooms, two baths home, and an acre of land, my career, my church, my community and important of all the youth, I left. As the director of the youth, in which I volunteered, I would drive through the neighborhood picking them up for choir rehearsal, sometimes making several trips to get them all. Bringing them home with me for ice cream and fresh lemonade. Joe wasn't involved in the church and would make accusations about the preacher and me. Once I missed the last three nights of the revival meeting because of these accusations but would not budge with my activities for the youths.

Our children, especially Laney needed constructive activities for the summer and I saw to it that they had by doing it myself. The boys were in little league, YMCA summer camp, and the planned activities at the church. It also gave me the opportunity to counsel with the teenage girls who were friends of Laney, who didn't think that I knew anything about anything. This was my way of keeping my children safe by keeping them close to me. Joe's abusiveness was beginning to include them, especially Joe the oldest boy. He was constantly telling them and me what he would do to them if they turned out to be "punks". Steve would ask me, "Mama what's a punk?"

Joe was six feet three inches and weighed one hundred –fifty pounds, maybe. He had the height but not the weight to play sports so he played through the boys. He always told them that football players don't cry. He would wrestle with the boys and they would get pretty rough at times; Lamont and Steve wouldn't cry but "Scooter" would. "Scooter" was a humble child who liked to play and not fight. Joe would threaten to beat him if he didn't fight. He would stand crying saying, "Daddy I don't want to fight, Joe would slap him. He was a prime target for Laney with her jealousy toward "Scooter" and me. She was always telling on him. She had taken his bed and gave her's to Claudia when she moved her into my home. It had been "Scooter" and I for a long time and now it's a house full. They all moved "Scooter" out of his place, my oldest child.

"Scooter" didn't breath on his own when he was borne. Dr. Pettis had to administer oxygen to get him breathing. "What's wrong with my baby, I was screaming, why he is not crying?" "Shirley take it easy I'm working to save this baby's life and I'll be with you in a minute," Dr. Pettis was saying. She had delivered several of Helen's children and knew the family well. Finally after what seemed to me an eternity, my baby began to cry. It's a miracle he's not cerebral palsy. That lack of oxygen for those seconds caused some awkwardness that is probable more noticeable to me than anyone else. I would work with him trying to teach him simple things until we both would become frustrated, and we both would be crying. I didn't know how to teach him. I discovered he could give back to me almost verbatim everything I'd read to him. He could pronounce the words, even large words, but could not associate the written word but could when he heard it. I tutored him for the military exam and he answered every question I asked. It didn't matter how it was asked, but failed the written test. He took the test again while in job corps. The recruiter said he had never witness a score as low as his. This has been a handicap for Joe and a lifetime of frustration form the molestation also, as well as the mental and physical abuse from his father.

Chante' Lamont Tugman was my "smart" child; he never crawled and walked at nine months, had his first two teeth at four month. I don't remember him not talking and making full sentences. He always spoke correct English. He talked as he heard me speak. I never talked baby talk to my children, I didn't understand it and I knew they wouldn't either. He was a fighter and demanded his place. He didn't take a lick off anyone especially his daddy. Joe would sleep with his arms over his face protecting it from Lamont. I never knew why Lamont would hit his daddy. It would always be when he's taking a nap or sleeping from working the third shift. Once he hit him with the clock radio, he actually climbed in bed with his daddy and lifted the radio from the headboard and dropped it on Joe's head. He would pick up a bowling trophy and hit him if he came through and Joe was sleeping on the couch. He would fight Laney also and he was only two years old. He's one of a few good men fighting in the United States Marine.

Lamont was eighteen months old when Steven was borne and was still in diapers and his bottle. He was very cautious with the new baby in the house. The day I came from the hospital with the new baby and put him in the crib where Lamont slept was an upsetting day for him. He cried all night, "That baby's in my bed." My friend Martha, who had four boys herself loaned me a crib for Steven. Steven was borne one month after I graduated from The School of

Cytology, Concord, NC. He was the most lovable baby I'd ever seen. He came here with his eyes wide opened and his hair looked as if it had been brushed; he was my miracle child. I dedicated him to God as I had promised.

Scooter was in school, Lamont and Steven were in the nursery, I was working at Rowan Memorial Hospital and Joe was doing his thing. He informed me early in the marriage that the children were my responsibility and not to expect him to keep them on his off days or vacation. I was supporting him, his daughter Laney, his sisters' daughter Claudia, and my three boys; I suffered from post- partum depression. I was physically, spiritually and emotionally tired. Two babies on bottles and in diapers, a teenager whose mother had just died, a rebellious stepdaughter and Joe's gambling and infidelity. It was this frame of mind I was in when I began working. It was my intentions to prepare to leave this miserable life and leave it all to Joe. I knew I had to make a change for the benefit of my boys. Steven had begun to stutter and regress in his speech pattern, Joe was wetting to bed and Lamont was becoming more insolent. Steven's stuttering stopped six months after we left Joe.

When I informed Joe of my plans to leave, his abuse accelerated. He thought he could bully me into staying. He threatened to kill the children and me nightly. He would come to bed about two in the morning, yank the covers off, and began to drill me as to who was I leaving him for. He had refused to go to counseling with me and even mocked me for going. "Why you going, he asked, to keep from committing suicide?" with laughter. "No, I replied coldly, to keep from committing homicide." He had never heard me speak to him in this manner, but this was a turning point for me. I had stayed as long as I did because I thought that I wasn't mentally strong enough to survive on my own neither was I prepared financially.

My career gave me the tools needed to survive. God knew my heart and my desire to serve him through serving humanity. The environment in which I was living was deplorable. My specialty assured me a position wherever there was a hospital. I had a teacher's certificate and had just finished a course at H&R Block's income tax school. It took the two jobs working sometimes as much as fourteen to sixteen hours a day to keep up my family of three growing boys. If only I had known how to trust in God how differently my destiny might have been. I had a desire to serve God as a small child and trusted him as a small child would. I called it, the voice my imaginary friend.

As I reminisce over my life these sixty plus years I can see God from the very beginning. My birth may have been a surprise to Ben and Helen but it was not a surprise or a mistake to God. He knew I would come into this world and He knew I would suffer the wrong all of my life just because of whom I am. The illegitimacy, the molestation, the rapes, the abortion, the abusive marriage and yes even being married to a homosexual; God saw it all.

"I've been through the fire, is how I've chosen to describe these last seven months in my life, and if someone had to go through what I endured why not me". Others would not have made it through the fire. God's been preparing me for these seven months sixty-three years. I'd suffered many different forms of persecution but nothing as this last one. Satan was determine to sift me as sand but greater is He that is in me than he that is in the world. Satan can never be

victorious over a Saint of the most- high God. After returning to Spartanburg and eventually married to Johnnie Lee Gray I found myself through The Church of Jesus Christ.

I had become so despondent with my life that I had had a second nervous breakdown, the first was living in Johnnies' mother's house with no inside facilities or water in the house. We had to go next door for water and use a "pot" to release yourself. When I married Johnnie I had a house, a car, and a job. He had nothing and six months after I married him I had nothing. I lost my house, my car was out of action because he had taken it to a bootlegged mechanic, and I was out of work as an insurance agent because I had no transportation. This place in life was becoming too familiar having left a home, a career, a community, and a church to get out of an abusive relationship with my children's father Joe and now married to a man that turned out to be another mouth to feed.

I knew nothing about Johnnie, his habits or his living condition. I was never able to answer the question my sons would ask, "Mama, why did you marry Johnnie?" I couldn't answer because I didn't know myself. Marriage wasn't in my plan; not even a serious relationship. My goal was to raise my three sons to be productive men. I had been separated from them for almost three years and was about to get them when Johnnie entered my life. He didn't have a clue how to be a father. He only had "papa", his granddaddy, as an example, papa was a drunk and so was Johnnie. Papa was known as "Gray" and Johnnie was "Gray Baby".

This man was unemployed more than he was employed and it didn't matter to him if he were unemployed. I kept wondering when he was going back to work. When I asked he had no job. He was involved with the state's rehabilitation system that dealt with the mentally challenged and drug and alcohol addicts. He had spent fifty-eight days in the Palmetto Center in Florence, SC and had been out for just a few days when he came to my home to do some work. I didn't know him but knew his partner Billy Anderson and trusted him for that reason only. He came and never left, sleeping with me every night as if he belonged in my home. In my childlike innocence I became subjective to this man and married him. He was looking for a home and an escape from poverty and found one in me.

He had been married once to a college classmate of mine that lasted for a year and a half and moved back with mama when it ended. There he had lived for nine years in the worst state of poverty, the only income being his mother's SSI check. I knew nothing of this nor anything else for that matter. I hired this man to do some work for me and three weeks later I am married to him. This marriage set me back twenty years. I worked hard to earn my way thru college. I worked sometimes two jobs to survive and support my children, now I had this man in my life. He was looking for some weak woman to take care of him, he found her in me.

My mother and sisters came to lecture but none told me what they knew about Johnnie Gray. My marriage to him lasted for twenty-one years ending in his death. It was twenty-one years of hell. He moved me from a three- bedroom house to a one- bedroom trailer with nothing working. I had become so depressed from losing my boys, losing my house and losing my job and now he moved me into his mama's house with no inside facilities; the house was filthy. His mother was in the hospital as she was two to three times a year. Her life was centered on her going to the doctor and going to the "horse'pital," she used it to control others in doing for her. The marriage was a farce.

The total recall of the molestation was a freeing of the mind and a releasing of years of pent-up frustration and anger. The nightmares began shortly after the marriage to Johnnie. I would wake up screaming and trembling with no explanation. I could never remember the dream that led up to the scream. I could only remember the pain and the fear of dying. It always felt as if I would die if I had not awakened when I did. Johnnie in the beginning would rush into the bedroom to see about me but they came so often that he began to dismiss them as "something Shirley does in her sleep. Moving me into his mother's house was more than my mind could take. We had been married nine months and I had had very little contact with my boys. When I called Joe and told him that I was married and wanted to bring the boys their clothes he dared me to come and told them that I was dead. I hated Johnnie for coming between my boys and me.

After I realized that he was not worried about working I encouraged him to pursue his gift as an artist. I continued to sell insurance and prepare income taxes. My career as a Cytotechnologist did not support us. Many times I would come in dog tired to a man who had never left the house but spent a day doing his own thing and it was not always painting. Throughout the twenty-one years Johnnie's earnings from various odd jobs and the sale of a few of his paintings benefited Johnnie and only Johnnie. The marriage gave him a place to call home and a place for his mother three weeks out of the month after she used and ate up everything her fifty dollars' worth of food stamps would buy.

I knew what was missing in my life and it was God. I had laid Him to the side and tried it on my own. I made a mess. June 6th, 1985, seven years into the marriage I found The Church of Jesus Christ. I was selling life insurance when I was introduced to Ruth Spruill, a young widow with three small children, who needed some insurance. It was the easiest sell ever made. I filled out the application with the answers she was giving me, when I asked for her beneficiary. "Nathan Peterkin," she answered. "Nathan Peterkin on the radio," I asked. "Yes, that's my dad, she said with pride. "Will I be collecting from his house or yours," I asked. "Daddy's please," she said shying away.

I had been listening to Brother Nathan Peterkin, ordained Evangelist of The Church of Jesus Christ for about three years on the Sunday morning gospel program at the local radio station. I was ecstatic to meet this man face to face. I had listened because he was someone who knew and understood the scriptures. I had had desired for some time to meet this man of God. I knew he was a man after God's own heart. The anointing spirit upon this man confirmed the spirit within me. I wanted to learn from him all that he knew about God. Meeting this man of God changed my life. I was full of questions. He gave me all of the answers directly from the word of God.

I had been church hopping for about a year when I decided they were all the same. Churches have become a business of making money rather than saving souls. It was refreshing to hear something different. I told him that I had prayed that God would send someone who knew the word of God and lived by the word of God. He was the answer to my prayers. He was stationed in Italy during the World War 1. There he met his bride Camilla and brought her back to New Jersey. They parented six children. Brother Nathan was the first person I had ever met and felt that I was in the presence of a holy man. He welcomed me, although Sister Camilla was a little jealous not only of him but her children also. He never tried to convert me to his faith and referred to the "Church" as the movement. I shared how I had listen to him faithfully and then turned him off for more than a year because of the bad reception, yet the station cleared up after he preached.

I had attended a charismatic church for seven years when I met Brother Nathan. I had more questions such as the evidence of the reception of the Holy Ghost is speaking in tongue. Dancing in the spirit, slain in the spirit and the trinity that was always confusing. We weren't allowed to ask questions about God. I wanted to be one of his students and asked if I might be. I brought Johnnie to meet him but he wasn't interested in knowing him at that time in his life. Later he said, "That man could see straight through him and he knew he was a true man of God." Meeting Ruth, his daughter, was the most important turning point in my life because I met God. I would listen to him introduce himself as Brother Nathan Peterkin, ordained Evangelist of The Church of Jesus Christ and would wait to hear the name of the church. The next week I would tune in a little earlier trying to hear the name of the church. I concluded that he just didn't give out the name.

While listening after a year I experienced the voice of the Lord asking me if I would feed His sheep. He asked me three times before I realized it was my call to be a servant for God. I answered, "Yes Lord I'll feed your sheep." I accepted this as a call to preach the gospel and began to make preparations to do a trial sermon. I returned to the Baptist Church where I been a member since I was eleven years old. They turned me down because I was a divorced and remarried woman. To preach in the Baptist Church would be against the rules of the Baptist Association. I appealed to my great aunt Della. She arranged for me to preach in the Methodist Church named after my great-granddaddy. I had my picture in the paper along with the announcement of my trial sermon. Thank God Brother Nathan say it in the paper. He and his family came to hear me. I asked him to close the service with a prayer. When he opened his mouth he was immediately recognized by the congregation for they too listened to the same radio station I listened to.

That one sermon was the beginning and ending of my preaching career from the pulpit and the beginning of my service to God. I was at Brother Nathan's house daily pumping him for more of the word of God. He shared many experiences with me but challenged me to not take his word but for me to ask God himself about his church. I was thrilled that I could ask God himself questions. Needless to say I asked him many.

Living is life experiences, whether they are positive or negative depends on your attitude of life. God does not work in negatives. For every evil there is a good. God loves us so much He gives us the liberty to choose. I chose to serve God to the best of my ability all the days of my life. God showed me His church and invited me to become a member of His body and I entered into His fold. When I entered the small-humbled building behind Brother Nathan's home, my eyes focused on the simple wood board, behind the simple built rostrum: <u>THE CHURCH OF JESUS CHRIST.</u> The understanding came immediately; this is the name of the church, The

Church of Jesus Christ. I knew my search was over, I had found what my spirit had longed for all of my life. The understanding brought with it wisdom and knowledge of an awesome God.

On June 6, 1985 Brother Arthur Scearcy baptized me into The Church of Jesus Christ. He drove seven hundred miles from Edison, New Jersey to baptize just one, me. Brothers and sisters drove all night, nine hours, to witness my covenant I made to my Lord and Savior Jesus Christ. We returned to the simple building where Brother Nathan laid hands on me for the reception of God's Holy Spirit and I became a new creature. As I returned to my seat my stomach harden on the right side, as it often did with much pain, and I began to experience a burning sensation and the harden stomach soften. I stood and shared the experience because God touched my body and healed me of an issue that had been there for many years. It would take me thirty to forty-five minutes to have a bowel movement because of the blockage yet when I returned home it took five flushes to eliminate all that came from my body. I know it was Colon cancer.

My spiritual growth flourished rapidly because of my hunger for the word of God. Sunday meeting and Wednesday night meetings did not satisfy my hunger. I asked Brother Nathan if he would come to my home for private teachings. He and Sister Camilla came every Monday morning. I would read chapters of scripture with an understanding I had never experienced. I would direct him throughout the community to the home of the sick and we would pray for them. He, Sister Camilla and I did this until he became too ill to drive. Brother Nathan died December 1987 but not before I became rooted me in The Church of Jesus Christ.

There have been many trials in life since Jesus Christ came into my life and we always come out victorious. Those who observe me call it luck but I know it's the blessings of God. I can see His hand in my life throughout all of the trials of life. My battles have not been with flesh and blood but with the powers and principalities of Satan. Having this knowledge how can you ever have hate in your heart against anyone instead of sorrow for their souls?

Johnnie had already begun drinking again before we moved to Arkwright, the land where I was born and grew up in. It was a humble house owned by Mr. Charles Atchison. As I stepped inside of the house I complained to God about how small it was and how dirty it was. I knew it was where I was supposed to be. The spirit said to walk around the premises seven times as the children of Israel did the Jericho wall so the wall of sin may fall from around this house and I did. Simple soap and hot water cleaned the walls of dirt and filth inside the house. People would come into my home and comment of the peace they felt while there. They would comment on how clean the house was. I further beautified it by planting flowers all around the house.

I had spent hundreds of dollars on attorney fees, days off work, and miles of driving back and forth to Salisbury to no avail in getting my children. When the courts did decide what to do about our children their father was awarded custody during school time and me during the summer time. I was devastated and slipped into a deep state of depression for months but when God stepped in it didn't cost a dime. My sons were now young handsome men, Joe was in Job Corp, Lamont was in the Marines and Steven was a senior at Spartan High School.

Brother Nathan taught us the battlefronts of life are world, family, church, and self and the greatest battle is self. I have been described as one who "buries the hatch but leaves the handle out." I have also been described as one with the memory of an elephant. These sayings describe an unforgiving person. "How can I forgive if you don't forgive?" The spirit spoke. "But Lord, look at all of the bad things they did to me," I argued. The spirit prompted me to write down the names and offenses on a sheet of paper. To my amazement there were over fifty names and the last were Brothers and Sisters of the church I had just met and some were dead. My list of offenses was nothing compared to the things in which I had done and was asking for forgiveness.

I fell to my knees and repented. I confessed to God that I didn't know how to forgive that he was going to have to do this for me. My greatest hurdle was my daddy. "Lord, I don't know why Ben don't like me, I've never done anything to him and he treats my children and I like outcast, he doesn't even want us in the house that I bought out of foreclosure so they could have a place to live." I argued. I could justify my hatred for Ben twenty-four seven, I also knew that it was something deeper than him just not liking me. God instructed me to pray for my daddy every day. It had to be a separated prayer from my daily prayer. Some mornings I would wake up justifying not praying for him. That would be my bad day until I stopped and said that special prayer for him. When I realized that the only person I could change was myself I became focus on what could I do to change me? I learned that just as Ben will be accountable for his actions so will I. I cannot control his actions but I can control my reaction. My concern became not whether Ben loved me or not but whether I loved Ben. I began to pray for myself that God would teach me how to forgive him and love him.

When his health began to fail him I would walk there in the morning and sit in his room. The first day he was throwing-up. I prepared him a glass of crushed ice with coke. I sat it on the nightstand next to his bed. He never touched it nor did he speak one word to me. I sat quietly and prayed silently as he lay in bed watching me. The phone rang, it was Elaine, "What you doing down there?" she asked. "I came to be here if Ben needs anything, I said. "Well, I'm sending Lita down there and you can leave," she said with a little aggravation in her voice. "That'll be fine because I need to get back home to work," I said as I got up to leave, "Ben I hope you get to feeling better, I'll be praying for you and I love you." I didn't wait for a response because I knew there would be none. The third morning I met him driving up the road, that devil couldn't stand to face my spirit another morning, I thought.

I returned home to finish sewing for this wedding of nine bridesmaids, two flower girls, and finishing up the bridal gown. I had not sewed in ten years. I had to leave my sewing machine in Salisbury when I left. There it was never closed and I sewed every day. I had prayed and asked God to give me something I could do at home to earn a living. I was burned out selling insurance. Each time I prayed the prayer I would be prompted to read Matthew 25. I read it for two weeks before I received the message in it for me. God had already blessed me with many talents and I had done as the one servant whom He gave one talent to, I had buried them. I said ok Lord I'll sew but I don't have a sewing machine. The same day a neighbor asked if I sewed and by the time I finished cutting out the pattern I had a sewing machine.

In a few days I'll be sixty-four years old and it is as if my life had just begun. For years it had been dictated by the needs of others before my needs. I had always been the "easy going will do anything for you type person." I would swallow a lot of insults and offenses and internalize them rather than speak up because I didn't want you to not like me. Being "liked" has been an emotion that plagued me all of my life.

OH where Oh where are my years?
Oh where oh where can they be?
We were born to die so when did I die?
I now feel alive.

Has my life been a lie or has the lie been my life?
The survivor struggle has ended and my living wasn't in vain.
God knew me before I knew myself for I was blessed from the womb.
Some called it a veil others a mask the covering of God.
My life wasn't a lie nor the lie my life.

Oh where oh where are my years?
I missed the little girl and grew up too soon.
The eyes of Satan, the author of lies, waited to devour.
The eyes of God, the author of truth, put me in his bosom.
He hid me from the evils of Satan and exposed his ways.
My life wasn't the lie and the lie wasn't my life.
For Satan is the lie but God is the truth.   Shirley Sims Gray September 10, 2005 ©